# A TREASURY OF TRADITIONAL TALES

Authors:

David Bowles, Frances Evans, AJ Eversole, Melissa-Jane Fogarty,
Anita Ganeri, Khaila Gentle, Neema Githere, Anika Hussain,
Ḵung Jaadee, Mariana Llanos, David Fa'auliuli Mamea,
Shirley Marr, Steph Matuku, Blessing Musariri, Marisa Paska,
Clifford Samuel, Mary Sebag-Montefiore, Zara Sekhavati, TuuP

Illustrator: Teo Georgiev
Publishing Director: Piers Pickard
Publisher: Rebecca Hunt
Editorial Director: Joe Fullman
Art Director: Andy Mansfield
Commissioning Editor: Kate Baker
Designer: Jade Wheaton
Print Production: Nigel Longuet

Published in September 2024
by Lonely Planet Global Limited
CRN: 554153
ISBN: 978-1-83758-301-0
1 3 5 7 9 10 8 6 4 2

Printed in Malaysia



Stay in Touch
Lonelyplanet.com/contact

Lonely Planet Office:

IRELAND
Digital Depot, Roe Lane (off Thomas St.), Digital Hub, Dublin 8, D08 TCV4, Ireland

MIX
Paper from responsible sources
FSC™ C021741

Paper in this book is certified against the Forest Stewardship Council™ standard. FSC™ promotes environmentally responsible, socially beneficial and economically viable management of the world"s forests.

lonely planet KIDS

# A TREASURY OF TRADITIONAL TALES

Retold by authors from around the world

Illustrated by

Teo Georgiev

# Contents

## Europe



## Asia



## Oceania

# Introduction

**Welcome, curious readers, to a treasure trove of traditional tales from around the world.** Many are from long, long ago, passed down through oral tradition. Generations of children have sat at the feet of their elders, listening to the extraordinary deeds of intrepid heroes and heroines, of dastardly villains, terrible monsters and mysterious beasts, talking animals, and magical beings that helped create and shape the world. Some stories help explain how things came to be or offer lessons in living your best life. Others are a warning against the dangers you might face, or are simply to entertain listeners on dark, gloomy nights. Together, they offer a glimpse into the memories, fears, and dreams of the people who first told them hundreds—or even thousands—of years ago.

# North America

The stories of North America include trickster tales of the First Nations peoples, Mexican creation myths, and spooky Caribbean legends of vampires and werewolves. Prepare to meet a shape-shifting raven that brings light to the world, a Cherokee medicine man who battles a colossal serpent, ape-like beasts that hide in the mountains of Mexico, and a mischievous forest spirit with backward-facing feet. Through these adventures, you'll learn about the importance of courage, cooperation, respect for nature, and the interconnectedness of all living things.

# Raven Brings Light to the World

## A Haida Tale
### Retold by K̲ung Jaadee

**Raven, also known as Yaahl, is one of the most** important supernatural beings in the stories of the Haida people of Canada. A trickster and shape-shifter, he created the world and all living things while flying around in the darkness for eons. His true form is that of a bird, but he can change his shape at will. When our story starts, everything was in darkness, until Raven used trickery to bring light to the world.

Long ago, the entire world was in complete darkness. It was cold all day and all night, making it difficult for people to move around or to gather and prepare food. Eventually, Raven's relatives, who lived in his village, started complaining.

"It's so cold all the time," said one.

"When I gathered food this morning, I couldn't see where I was going, and I tripped and spilled all the berries!" said another.

"When I was pulling in my fishing net, I fell overboard, and I was wet all day."

They surrounded Raven, who was now in his human form, and started pulling on his arms and begging him to help them.

"How can I help?" Raven asked.

"There's a greedy chief who keeps the

great ball of light inside a large box in his house," one relative began. "He's so stingy, he won't even let his family see it!"

Another blurted, "Raven! You can go and get a piece of the light so we can use it when we're gathering food. We'll be safe and dry, and we'll be warm!"

Raven realized he too was tired of tripping around in the darkness, so he changed into the great bird that he is and flew toward the chief's village. He knew that every now and then, the greedy chief would peek inside his box to make sure the light was still in there, then quickly slam the lid shut so no one could see it.

So, Raven circled the village, looking carefully at the houses, searching for a sign. After a while, he noticed a flash of light coming from inside one house. It lasted only a moment, but it was enough.

"Ah ha! That's it!" Raven cried. He flew down and tapped on the door.

Meanwhile, watching from a branch on a tall snag (dead tree) nearby, was Eagle —a supernatural being and powerful hunter known for his keen eyesight.

*Well, well, well, if it isn't Raven! I'd better watch him carefully. He's likely to get into trouble!* thought Eagle.

Answering the knock on the door, the chief invited Raven to come inside and sit beside him, then served him some freshly cooked salmon with some fresh water to drink.

Once his guest had finished eating, the chief asked him, "Raven, why are you here in my house? What do you want from me?"

"Chief! I'm so glad you've asked me!" replied Raven. "I have come from a village far from here, and my relatives and I are tired of tripping around in the darkness. We're tired of being cold all the time. We all heard about your great ball of light. We're wondering if you can give us a small piece of it so we can safely gather our food and warm ourselves?"

The chief stood up, his face turned bright red, and his hands clenched into fists.

"You get out of my house immediately! Never return! How dare you ask such a question!" he shouted.

**"This light belongs to ME! GET OUT! GET OUT NOW!"**

Raven realized the chief would not change his mind. He peered into the darkness and now noticed a young woman sitting on the other side of the chief. He could tell from the shape of her nose and mouth that she was the chief's daughter. Perhaps she could help him find the light?

He walked out the door and hid in the bushes nearby. He wanted to stay close to the house to see which job the young woman would do to help her relatives. In the village, everyone did something to contribute.

Raven was rewarded the next morning, when he noticed she got up early and walked to the stream, where the water was cold and fresh. She dipped a bucket into the stream, filled it, and went back to the house.

The following morning, Raven waited upstream from where she had dipped her bucket, and as soon as she placed it in the stream, he immediately changed himself into a tiny spruce needle. He dropped himself into the water and floated right into her bucket. By using his special magic, he made her so thirsty that she picked the bucket up and drank all the water down. She was surprised to be that thirsty but was grateful to still be at the stream so she could refill her bucket.

Afterward, she went into the house. Little did she know, she had swallowed the spruce needle, which really was Raven.

While babies usually take nine months to grow, this baby wasn't like that.

After just two weeks, the young woman grew as big as though she had swallowed the Moon.

"Why has my daughter become so big?" wondered the chief. He couldn't see her clearly, but he had noticed that it took him much longer to move around her than before. Right at that moment a baby slipped out of her body, and into her arms.

"Dad?"

"Yes, my daughter?"

"I just had a baby!" she blurted out in surprise.

**"WHAT?! A BABY?! HOW ON EARTH . . . ?" he cried angrily.**

His daughter quickly placed the newborn into his arms. He stopped being angry as he peered into the darkness where his new grandchild was starting to cry.

"I am a grandfather!" he yelled. He ran to every relative in the house and to everyone in the village. He invited them all to give his new grandson a welcome kiss. Each person bent toward the little bundle. They were about to kiss the baby when they stopped themselves. Instead of soft baby skin, they felt rough hair, like feathers, brush against their face.

They made excuses: "I must go pull in my fishing net," said one.

"The berries are ripe, and I'm going to pick them," added another.

No one kissed the baby, but the chief didn't notice that. He loved his grandson enough for everyone in the whole world.

The baby grew really quickly. After two weeks, he was running around like a two-year-old. Soon, he was saying his first words, "Give it to me, Grandpa. Give it to me."

The chief gave his grandson everything he asked for. The new mother tried to stop her father.

"Dad, no, don't let him have that… Oh I give up."

Really, the little Raven child was snooping around, trying to find the box that held the great ball of light.

One day, while the grandson was playing, he found an enormous box under his grandfather's bed. It was the biggest box in the house. Since he knew what it was right away, he asked his grandfather if he could play with it. He was stunned when his grandfather told him he could not, because he usually gave him whatever he wanted.

The boy began to cry, his wails growing louder and louder until the chief called out to his daughter, "Let my grandson play with the light for a little while. I must lay down. My head hurts."

The daughter led the boy to the enormous box and he opened it, slowly. The great ball of light shone so nicely.

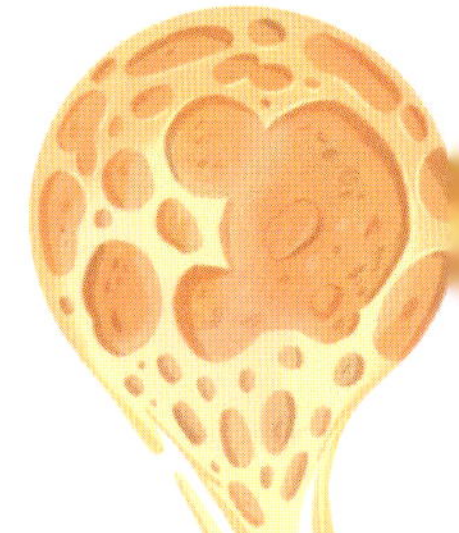

He lifted the light out of the box, then tossed it into the air and caught it over and over again. He bounced the ball throughout the house, then put it on the floor and started kicking and chasing it around. He laughed gleefully, thrilled he had the light at last.

Then he kicked the light into a corner, leaving himself in darkness once more. While hidden, he changed back into his great Raven shape. He picked the light up with his beak and flew out through the smoke hole into the sky. (Some say that the great light scorched Raven's beak and feathers black, and this is how all ravens became all black; before this moment, they were white.)

The chief sat up in bed, and noticing the empty box, he shouted, "Hey! Where's my light?"

He jumped out of bed and as he ran out of the door, he saw Raven flying away with the light in his beak.

"Raven! Come back with my light, you thief, you!"

Eagle, still sitting in his tree close to the house, watched as Raven sped past him. *I had better get that light from Raven*, he thought to himself. *I knew when he arrived he was up to mischief*.

Eagle flew fast toward Raven and grabbed one side of the light in his beak. Raven held fast onto the other side of the light. Eagle pulled harder.

They were having a tug-of-war in the sky, pulling this way and that, when, all of a sudden, the light started breaking into pieces.

It broke into a big piece—the Sun.

It broke into a smaller piece—the Moon. And it broke into a lot of smaller pieces—the stars.

"My light, my light!" cried the chief in dismay. But then he felt the warmth of the Sun and saw how happy everyone was.

"Well, I guess my light is in a better place after all," he said.

And this is the story of how Raven brought light to the world. It is a reminder for us to share what we have with others. If someone needs something that we have, then we can share to help others.

**Author's note**

This is my retelling of a popular cultural story from the X̱aayda (Haida) people passed on to me by my uncle T. Richard Baker through our oral storytelling tradition and also includes some fictional elements.

# The Uktena's Diamond

## A Cherokee Tale
## Retold by AJ Eversole

**In Cherokee folklore, the Uktena is a colossal serpent** with great pointed horns upon its head. It has a thick body as wide as a tree trunk, and scales that glint like small mirrors, stunning those who look its way. However, none of these are the most defining feature of the Uktena. Instead, it is best known for the giant iridescent diamond called the Ulunsuti that rests between its eyes. It is said that those who possess the Ulunsuti will have all their desires come true.

Many years ago, in the southeastern woodlands of what is now the United States, the Cherokee people dwelled. In that time, they referred to themselves as the Aniyvwiya (a-nee-yuh-we-ya), or "real people." Their forests were lush and full of life, their rivers wide, and fish plentiful.

One day, the Sun looked down upon them. She tried to meet their eyes, but the people would only scrunch their faces and frown. Their reaction offended her. She complained to her brother, the Moon, who loved the Aniyvwiya.

"But they're beautiful," he said. "They look up at me in peace. They enjoy my milder light."

The Sun was jealous of her brother, and her fury could not be contained. The angrier she grew, the hotter she became, and the hotter she became, the more that people frowned. A vicious cycle took hold. The autumn crops withered under her glare, the grass that was once glorious green turned into cracking yellow blades, and the rivers shrank in size to avoid her.

In an effort to stop her, the Aniyvwiya begged the Yunwi Tsunsdi, a tribe of nature spirits that took the shape of Little People, for help.

"We must destroy the Sun, before she destroys us," said the Aniyvwiya, and so the Little People took two of the Aniyvwiya and magicked them into giant serpents: one a rattlesnake, the other a horned serpent called an Uktena. The creatures had been created to kill the Sun and raced against each other to complete their job.

The rattlesnake beat the Uktena to the Sun, who dwelled in her daughter's house. It coiled, with its long fangs ready to strike, and began to shake its tail to lure the Sun out.

The door opened and it struck! But it wasn't the Sun who had answered the door; it was her daughter. She immediately fell dead in the doorway.

The Sun was so overcome with grief that she began to sob great gushing tears onto the Earth. This restored the water to the dried lakes, quenched the thirst of the people, and cooled off the land.

The rattlesnake became the feared and respected chief of the snake tribe, while the Uktena entered into a deep rage for failing to accomplish the task it was created for. It became bitter and unapproachable and would use its mirrored scales to blind anyone who came near. On other occasions, it would allow curious passers-by to admire the shine of its scales in order to draw them closer, before striking.

---

**The Aniyvwiya deemed the Uktena too dangerous to exist.**

---

They banished it away from the tribe, out to a lonely existence in the wilderness.

There the Uktena built its nests in the deepest crevices within the caves and bluffs, along pools of water rarely visited, and on dark winding passes in the tallest mountains. It rested for long periods of time, often sleeping for years undisturbed. It was not unheard of for dirt and leaves to accumulate on top of the Uktena and for its horns to be mistaken for the branches of a young tree. While it rested, it dreamed of revenge. All the while, its resentment for the Aniyvwiya grew and grew.

There became a great legend passed down through the tribal clans that whoever killed the Uktena or its offspring and claimed the glimmering diamond, Ulunsuti, would be granted any wish they desired. Few encountered an Uktena and lived to tell the tale. But there was one who had managed to escape the monstrous serpent and relay what he had learned. He claimed that the Uktena's scales were as hard as stone and shone bright under any light, be it the Sun or the Moon. Its coloring was ringed, like a kingsnake, and underneath the seventh ring from its horns was its heart. Strike the underside of this seventh ring and the Uktena would die. He also learned that its blood was filled with a powerful poison that killed all living things it touched.

Now there is only one person known to have ever defeated an Uktena. While warring with an enemy tribe of magicians, the Aniyvwiya managed to capture a great medicine man named Aganunitsi.

"Please," he begged, "spare me and I will defeat the Uktena for you. I will give you the Ulunsuti and all your wishes will be granted."

"Who do you think you are?" one of them asked him. "You think you can not only find the beast, but kill it as well? It is an impossible task. You will surely die."

"I will die here amongst you or fighting against the Uktena," replied Aganunitsi.

> **"What is the harm in letting me try?"**

They scoffed at him but found no fault in his logic. They released him under the condition that he do nothing but hunt for the Uktena. There would be no second chances if he strayed from his purpose.

Aganunitsi left for what is now called the Great Smoky Mountains to hunt for the creature. Along the way, he discovered countless fantastical beasts long thought to be creatures of myth. Their hides alone would fetch him fame and glory, but he left them alone and continued on his quest. He came across the enchanted Lake Atagahi, known for its healing waters, but he merely slept on its bank before leaving it behind without investigation.

As he hunted, Aganunitsi came up with a strategy. He knew he did not need his magic to defeat the beast, just the bow and arrow he'd been trained to use as a child and his own courage. If his aim was true, he would pierce the heart.

After searching east, west, and north, he finally turned south toward the Gahuti mountain, where he happened upon the sleeping beast before realizing it. Luckily, his rustling did not wake it. He scouted the area. They were midway up the mountain, where sparse trees littered the slope and the brush had been blown down by the Uktena's breathing through its large nostrils. At the bottom of the ravine was a twisting river.

Aganunitsi began to set his plan into action. First, he dug a trench a little way down the mountainside from the sleeping Uktena. He filled it with pinecones and set them alight, making sure the fire was blazing before climbing back up the slope toward the beast.

He slowly drew his bow, carefully taking aim at the seventh ring. He loosed the arrow and it struck true!

The Uktena reared upward, startled, then swung its massive head to face Aganunitsi. The Ulunsuti on its forehead came to life in a great burst of light.

Aganunitsi quickly ran down the

slope and leapt over his line of fire. All the while, the Uktena pursued him, intent that if it were to die, it would take Aganunitsi with him. As it moved, blood poured from its wound, killing all living things in its path. Leaves and trees withered, burned through to smoking husks.

As it reached Aganunitsi, it let out a piercing scream, blood pouring from its wound. As the blood touched the fire, it sizzled and dissipated. The poison within it was rendered useless.

Soon, the dying monster could not defy gravity any longer. Its body collapsed and rolled down the hill, crushing every tree in its path. It came to rest by the riverbank. Aganunitsi called forth the birds to come and feast upon its body. Seven days later, he returned to the site

and found nothing but bones.

Ravens are drawn to shiny things, and one could not resist the temptation of trying to take the Ulunsuti, but the stone was too big and had been dropped not far from the remains, which is where Aganunitsi found it.

When he picked up his prize, Aganunitsi instantly knew it should not be handed over to anyone else. The Uktena had rested for a long time, and its dreams had bled into the stone, filling it with resentment. It was a powerful object indeed, but heavy with dark magic.

He returned to the Aniyvwiya. At first, they did not believe his story, insisting on seeing the stone themselves. He took it from the deerskin he had wrapped it in. When they saw it, they, too, felt nothing but dread. They told him to take it from the village and keep it somewhere far away.

Aganunitsi listened to them and hid it in a cave a day's journey from the village, safe from the hands of anyone who might misuse its power. Every seven days, he fed it by rubbing it with the blood of an animal, and twice a year, he even fed it his own blood in order to try and tame the resentment.

Over time, the stone brought Aganunitsi great wisdom, despite its dark magic. He could use it to foresee the outcome of a war, whether a sick person might recover, or even the time of a person's death. No other medicine man ever became as powerful as Aganunitsi. And when he died, the Aniyvwiya buried the Ulunsuti with him, so that it might never be used for wicked purposes against the tribe. His burial site has remained a closely guarded secret by the Aniyvwiya ever since.

# Sisimites

## A Tale from Mexico
## Retold by David Bowles

**For centuries, the people of Central America and** Southern Mexico have glimpsed a huge, hairy creature in the jungles and mountains. It goes by many names, but the most common is Sisimite, which comes from the Nahuatl word *tzitzimitl*, meaning "monster." Some people believe these Sisimites to be relatives of the Bigfoot, Sasquatch, or Yeti—wild animals, unknown to science. But the Indigenous peoples of Mesoamerica (ancient Mexico and Central America) have described a different origin for these creatures—one that goes right back to the creation of the Earth.

According to the Nahua and Maya, the gods had tried to make the world and its people several times. Each attempt was a little better than the last, but they all ended in almost total ruin at the hands of the God of Destruction and Chaos—also known as Hurricane, or the Smoking Mirror. However, each time, small remnants survived with the help of Hurricane's brother and rival, Feathered Serpent, God of Creation and Order.

During the First Age, the world was inhabited by giant people and creatures. One day, Hurricane sent enormous jaguars to gobble up all the people.

"Why, brother?" demanded Feathered

Serpent, after hiding the survivors in a cave. "We made these people together!"

"Because they love you more," Hurricane snarled. "They never sing praises to me."

Then the brothers fought, and their struggle destroyed the Earth. Finally, Feathered Serpent gripped his brother and hurled him far away into the cosmos, declaring him banished.

So began the Second Age. Feathered Serpent and the demigods of nature remade the world even more beautiful than before. New people were created, and they said prayers of thanksgiving to their Creator under the watchful eye of giants, the survivors of the First Age.

After many years, a dark spot began to grow on the horizon, worrying the people.

"Have mercy, Feathered Serpent!" they cried out. "Our doom approaches fast!"

But it was too late. Hurricane had returned, furious at his brother's new creation. Spinning across the vast cosmic sea, he slammed his great arms of wind and rain against the world, knocking down buildings and sending people flying into the void.

Feathered Serpent managed to save a handful of men and women from this deadly storm by transforming them into apes with tails. They clung fearfully to deep-rooted trees, while Feathered Serpent spoke to his brother, hoping to calm him and strike a bargain.

"Let us try once more," Feathered Serpent said. "But this time, some other god can rule the Earth so that neither you nor I get all the praise."

Jealous Hurricane agreed. When the winds died down, the brothers remade the Earth, and the God of Rain took their place in the heavens.

Meanwhile, the talking apes retreated into the deep shadows of the forests. Could descendants of these

survivors exist even now, during our modern age? That's what many Indigenous peoples claim. Over the years, numerous tourists have tried and failed to prove the creatures' existence.

Still, some have come away with a story to tell. Like the Castillo family.

The Castillos loved adventure. So, when their daughter, Ana, turned twelve, Ed and Susan Castillo gave her a special graduation gift: a family trip to Mexico's most famous volcanoes: Iztaccíhuatl and Popocatépetl.

After flying to Mexico City, the Castillos rented a car and drove to the town of Amecameca, watching in awe as the outlines of the volcanoes grew larger.

After settling in, they met with their guide, Nestor Pérez.

"Just call me Nieves," he said with a smile. Ana laughed, because *nieve* in Spanish means "snow."

"How long will it take?" Ana's mother asked.

"Nearly all day," Nieves explained. "The ascent is a pretty easy walk over scree and snow slopes—not too much of a challenge. But Popo can be unforgiving if you get careless, so stick to the rules, and obey my team at all times."

Once the climbing began, Nieves took the lead as they gradually zigged and

zagged up the volcano's slope.

After about three hundred yards, the group took a long break. Ana chatted with the members of Nieves's team before asking about the volcano's name.

"Ah, surely you've heard the story?" Nieves exclaimed.

Ana shrugged. "All I know is that Popocatépetl means 'smoking mountain' and that it erupts out of anger."

Nieves shook his head. "Not anger. Sadness. He was a Toltec warrior, long ago. The king promised the hand of his daughter in marriage to whoever could lead their army to victory against the enemy. Popoca, the secret love of the princess, took charge and won the war. But a jealous rival came back early and reported that the warrior had fallen. Out of grief and loss, the princess took her own life."

"Ah," said Ana softly. "So when Popoca returned, he found her dead."

"Yes. He carried her body into the mountains and cried out to the gods, who transformed the pair into two volcanoes. The princess is Iztaccíhuatl, 'the white woman,' blanketed in snow and sleeping forever. But Popocatépetl is a seething cauldron of sorrow."

Reflecting on the story, the Castillos continued their climb, soon reaching freshly fallen snow broken here and there by black rock. The incline was steeper, and no word was said amidst grunts and pants until Ana saw something impossible.

## "Look at the size of this footprint!"

she called out in alarm.

Everyone crowded around and stared at the track, nearly two feet long and some eight inches wide, narrowing at the heel.

Several of the guides began to mutter. Three of them walked a little farther, finding a long trail of prints.

"Sisimites," one muttered, crossing himself.

Ana's father turned to their guide. "What does this mean?"

Nieves gestured at the climbers. "We need to get off this mountain. Now."

Ana's mother let out a scream, pointing at an outcropping fifty yards away.

Everyone turned.

Two massive figures were rushing their way up the glacier, their broad feet propelling them in inhuman bounds over the snow. Ana yanked her phone from her pocket and began to film them. One of the dark, hairy creatures paused and turned.

Its nostrils widened as it sniffed the frigid air. A strange growl thrummed along the ice beneath their feet as it narrowed its eyes.

"Move!" shouted Nieves. "This trip is over!"

In a panic, the Castillos went skidding over snow and rock and ice. From behind them came the thud of a flare gun. Ana turned to see the monsters climbing fast, covering ground in minutes that humans would have needed hours to cross. The creatures' towering, furry forms went red beneath the flare for a second, and then they were lost in the distant mist.

The entire family was shell-shocked, but the sighting especially haunted Ana Castillo for months afterward. She remembered the word "Sisimite" and read all she could find about the legendary creature. And as she watched the blurry video she had captured, Ana came to realize something important. The creature that had turned was the bigger of the two. It had seen the phone in her hands and thought she was a threat.

"He was protecting his mate. We were in their territory," she whispered. "The real Popocatépetl and Iztaccíhuatl."

Then she canceled the upload to her social media.

*They deserve their privacy*, she thought. But she didn't delete the video.

# Tata Duende

## A Tale from Belize
Retold by Khaila Gentle

**If you find yourself in the jungle of Belize and hear** whistling in the middle of the night, it could mean that Tata Duende is near. At just three feet tall, with his feet turned backward, this mischievous spirit is said to love stealing thumbs. Those who wander too far from home, especially curious children, are at risk of being carried away by him. Find a way to outsmart Tata Duende, though, and you might learn that there is also a kind side to this mysterious forest dweller.

Long ago, deep in the heart of Belize's rainforests, there was a small village called Blue Creek, named after the sparkling blue-green waters of a tiny river that ran nearby. The village sat hidden away in the foothills of Belize's rolling green mountains, surrounded by tall broadleaf forests that were home to all sorts of amazing wildlife, from jaguars and tapirs to scarlet macaws and howler monkeys.

Living in Blue Creek was a young boy named Edwardo. Although Edwardo had grown up with the rainforest right in his backyard, the thought of the forest sometimes made him fearful. To him, it was a dark, wet place that held countless scary creatures just waiting to jump on people.

One night, when he and his family were just about finished eating supper, he turned to his mother and asked, "Why do we have to live so close to the forest? Why don't we just cut down the trees so that the forest is farther away?"

His mother looked at him, smiling, and replied, "Because, dear Edwardo, we're supposed to live in harmony with the forest—like we have for many, many years now. Cutting down more than we should will do much more harm than good." She placed a gentle hand under his chin and added, teasingly, "Besides, most of the animals in the forest are more afraid of us than we are of them."

She then got up, clearing everyone's plates and taking them to the washbowl. "There's nothing to be afraid of out there, my sweet boy."

"That's not true," Edwardo's older sister chimed in after their mother walked away. "Tata Duende lives in the forest. And you should *definitely* be afraid of him."

Edwardo's brows perked up with curiosity. "Why?" he asked, having never heard of a Tata Duende before.

"Go out into the forest alone, and he will steal you away. And if he sees your thumbs, he will chop them off and steal those too!" As she said this, she suddenly raised her voice, startling Edwardo.

"You know better than to tell your brother scary stories before bedtime, Kaia. Now, both of you go brush your teeth and get ready for bed," said their mother as she shooed them from the kitchen.

As Kaia and Edwardo stood outside brushing their teeth, Edwardo noticed just how dark the night was. A single oil lamp hanging above their heads was the only source of light. It illuminated the side of their little wooden house and not much else. He paused, and with his cup and toothbrush in his hands, he listened to the sounds of the night. The wind blowing through the forest sounded like rain, and there was also the quiet chirping of insects and toads.

"You know," Kaia said, "they say that if you hear whistling in the night, it means Tata Duende is near."

"You're lying," Edwardo replied.

"It's true!" Kaia insisted. "He loves to play tricks on people. But don't be fooled —just remember this: if the whistling sounds close, then Tata Duende is in fact very far away and you have time to escape. If his whistling sounds far away, though, that means he's nearby and he could pounce at any moment."

Just then, their mother called them inside—it was time for bed.

For a long time after his conversation with his sister, Edwardo couldn't stop thinking about Tata Duende. One night, about a week later, he lay in his hammock about to fall asleep, when suddenly, he heard a loud whistle. It pierced the silence of the night, and it sounded like it was coming from right there in his room.

He shot up from where he lay, his heart pounding loudly in his chest. He expected to see Kaia standing there, having played a prank on him, but there was no one.

Then, there was another loud whistle, this time coming from outside his room.

---

**He gasped, his eyes wide with fright.**

---

Still convinced that it was Kaia, he quietly slid out of his hammock and tiptoed his way across the house.

*It can't be*, he thought to himself. *Tata Duende is not real!*

When he got to his sister's room, Edwardo saw Kaia seemingly asleep. Suddenly, the whistling began again. This time, it didn't stop, and it sounded like it was coming from right outside the house. Kaia didn't move, and Edwardo realized that she really was fast asleep.

*Maybe it's a bird, or some other creature from the rainforest that's making the noise,* he thought.

Edwardo turned and looked at the door that led outside. Grabbing the slingshot his father had given him for his birthday that year, he slipped quietly out of the house. He was determined to prove that Tata Duende wasn't real.

Guided by the light of the full Moon, and the whistling that seemed to grow quieter and farther away, Edwardo reached the edge of the forest, his heart thumping loudly in his chest. Behind him, he could see the thatched roof of his home off in the distance. Meanwhile, tall mahogany and ceiba trees towered over him, making him feel like an ant. At that moment, he heard the soft hooting of an owl and looked up just in time to notice one fly overhead and disappear behind the trees. When he gazed back down, he jumped at the sight before him. Looking up at Edwardo, with a frown on his wrinkled face, was a man about three feet tall.

The man wore tattered old clothes that covered most of his body, except for his feet, which were turned backward, and his hands, which had no thumbs. He also wore a wide-brimmed straw hat that seemed too big for his head, and he held on to an old and twisted wooden staff. Edwardo's strong resolve to prove that Tata Duende wasn't real suddenly vanished, for there he was, standing right in front of him.

"What business do you have in my forest, boy?" Tata Duende spoke up, his voice booming.

When Edwardo didn't answer, the forest spirit grew annoyed, striking the ground with his staff. "Are you a hunter, or are you a logger? Which is it?"

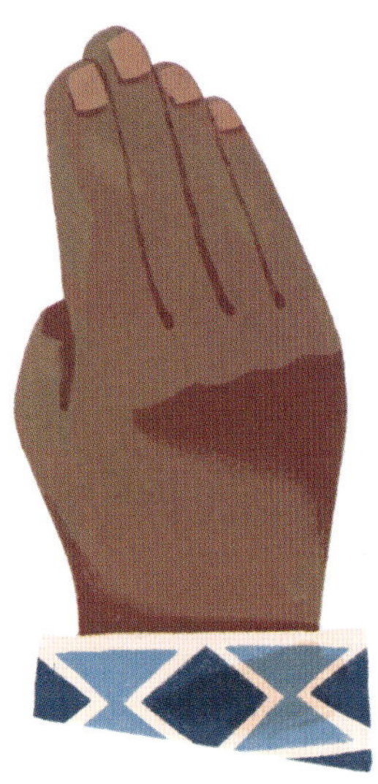

In shock, Edwardo took two steps back, dropping his slingshot. Tata Duende watched as it fell to the ground, and then added, "Are you here to bring the forest harm?"

The spirit stepped closer, looking up at Edwardo with narrowed eyes. "Quickly," he said. "Show me your hands."

Trembling, Edwardo began to raise his hands when he remembered his sister's words:

**"If he sees your thumbs, then he'll steal those too."**

Edwardo quickly folded his thumbs into his palms and showed the forest spirit the back of his hands instead of the front. Then, he replied, softly, "I am neither of those things."

Tata Duende examined Edwardo's hands. Then, he said, "If what you say is true, then tell me, what is one way that humans can live in harmony with the forest?"

For a moment, Edwardo froze, his mind blank. But then, he remembered what his mother often told him.

"By not cutting down more than we should," he said. Feeling confident now, he added, "And maybe even planting more trees to replace what we cut down."

Slowly, Tata Duende's mean old frown

disappeared. He gave a slight smile and uttered a thoughtful, "Hmm." It was only as the forest spirit's smile grew that Edwardo became sure that his trick had worked.

"Then you must be lost," Tata Duende said. "Come, let me show you the way home."

With his fear subsiding, Edwardo decided to follow, keeping his thumbs tucked away tightly in his fists.

Along the way, Tata Duende muttered, "Those blasted loggers and hunters. They cut down the trees and leave nothing behind. They kill the jaguars and the deer without a second thought. I'll have none of that in my forest."

As they neared his home, Edwardo told Tata Duende about his sister's scary story. The spirit laughed loudly.

"Well, next time someone tries to tell you about me tell them this: only those who seek to bring the forest harm have reason to fear me."

After quietly opening the door, Edwardo turned to say goodbye, but the spirit had vanished.

Edwardo scanned the area for any sign of him, but there was nothing—only the forest which, for the first time, Edwardo saw as beautiful.

The story of Edwardo's encounter quickly spread. Now, anyone who comes across Tata Duende knows to cleverly hide their thumbs, and everyone knows that although he may seem scary,

---

**Tata Duende is, first and foremost, a guardian of the forest.**

---

# South America

From the thrilling myths of the Inca to colorful legends from the Brazilian rainforest, the stories of South America reveal the traditions and beliefs of its Indigenous peoples, blended with those of its European and African communities. In this collection, you'll encounter gods and goddesses doing battle on the towering peaks of the Andes Mountains, meet a vengeful mermaid, and venture under the sea and beyond this world into the afterlife.

# Nine-Night

## A Tale from Guyana
## Retold by TuuP

**Nine-Night is a tradition from Africa practiced** throughout the Caribbean and beyond. On the ninth night after a person's passing, friends and family gather for a great celebration with singing, storytelling, dancing, and feasting to make sure the dead person's spirit can move on to the next life and does not come back to haunt the living. But letting go of our loved ones isn't always easy . . .

There was once a young girl named Kwanza, who lived in the small village of Buxton-Friendship on the coast of Guyana, along with her mother and father, Minky and Ivern, and her grandmother, Ida. One sad night, Kwanza's beloved grandmother passed away. Kwanza was heartbroken.

"Listen, Kwanza," Minky said gently, "I know you loved your granny dearly, and she loved you in return. Tomorrow we will start getting her ready for the next world."

"What world is that?" Kwanza asked.

"The world of our ancestors," replied Minky. "Would you like to give us something to leave with your grandmother as your parting gift?"

Kwanza thought for a moment, then walked over to a shelf where a painted stone rested. She brought it to her mother, saying, "I liked the shape of this stone that I found and I wanted to paint it. Granny Ida helped me choose the colors. She said they reminded her of a

scarlet macaw. She told me that whenever I'm lonely, I can take out the stone and think of her."

Minky took the stone and hurried Kwanza to bed. In the morning, Ivern and Minky went to dress Granny Ida. She was laid out in all her finery, with Guyanese gold earrings and rings. Then they called Kwanza in, as promised.

**She placed the brightly painted stone in her grandmother's palm.**

Later that day, Ida was laid to rest.

As the days passed, there was a buzz amongst the villagers in anticipation of the Nine-Night celebrations. They wanted to give Kwanza's grandmother a good send-off, as she was a kindhearted woman who always wore a smile on her face, and she was loved by all.

On the morning of the eighth day, preparations began. Food was laid out, and decorations and flowers strung up. As the Sun set, people started to gather. The Moon shone its face, and the warm tropical night embraced all the well-wishers. The yard thronged with people who had come from all over the three Guianas—Guyana, Suriname, and French Guyana—and from the jungle interior, too. Some had even traveled from across the Caribbean Sea to the little village of Buxton-Friendship.

By the evening of the ninth day, the time had come for Kwanza's parents to pour water from the calabash bowl onto the ground, offering up libations to the ancestors—to those who had gone before—so that the Nine-Night could begin. But the family was nowhere to be seen.

The master drummer, whose name was Cuffy, climbed the wooden steps leading to the family's home and knocked on the front door. On the third knock, the door slowly opened and Ivern peered out.

"Kwanza won't leave the house," he confessed. "She hasn't spoken a word or eaten a thing since we laid her grandmother to rest. She doesn't want any of you to be here. Please go home; there will be no Nine-Night tonight."

"Ivern," Cuffy said gently. "See how many people have come to honor Grandmother, for she was grandmother to us all, and we all loved her. But this is how we do things. This is the way it has always been done."

"Remember," he continued, "we only

stay for a while on Earth until we must move on. Grandmother is on her journey to the land of our ancestors. We don't want her to be trapped in limbo, forever wandering between this world and the next."

"I know," replied Ivern. "But we're not ready."

"May I speak with Kwanza?" Cuffy asked.

Kwanza heard her name being called and came to the front door. Cuffy smiled and said calmly, "Look at all the people who loved your dear Granny Ida. Do you really want to send them away?"

Kwanza looked Cuffy in the eyes and replied, "Master drummer, can't you bring me Grandmother back?" Ivern and Minky were amazed to hear their daughter talk after so many days of silence.

"It's not as easy as that," replied Cuffy.

"Then you are not who you say you are!" replied Kwanza and walked away.

"OK," said Cuffy gently. "I go talk with Grandmother and see what she got to say about the matter."

"Did Cuffy say he was going to speak with Grandmother?" whispered one of the villagers. "How can that be?"

Cuffy picked up his drum, beating a rhythm as he walked away from the house and out of the village. First, the children began to follow Cuffy, and then some adults. People shouted out, "Drummer-man, what's going on!" But Cuffy just kept walking.

By now, a crowd was following behind Cuffy as if he were leading a Mashramani carnival procession. They did not know where they were going, but Cuffy walked with such grace and determination that the crowd could not help but follow the rhythm of the drum all the way to the beach. There, they stood, by a sandy bank, looking out at the sea.

Still Cuffy kept drumming as he walked into the water. Waves washed at his feet, then his knees, then his waist.

"De man mad. What's going on!" cried an onlooker.

The water was now up to Cuffy's neck. Then the waves took him under, and he was gone. The crowd looked on in disbelief as they heard the distant sound of Cuffy's drum, still beating out a rhythm.

Cuffy, now under the sea, continued walking and walking until he came to the land of the departed—another place of existence, there, beneath the waves. Up ahead was a bustling market. Cuffy approached one of the traders and asked if they knew of a new arrival known as Grandmother, from the village of Buxton-Friendship. The trader pointed toward a stall laden with all kinds of fruits: apple, bananas, mangoes, soursop, noni, pawpaw, sori, guinep, five finger star apple, coconut, and breadfruit. As Cuffy got near, he could see Grandmother was talking and laughing.

"Grandmother!" he said.

Grandmother looked at Cuffy with surprise. "Cuffy, you pass over. When you deceased?" she asked.

"No," replied Cuffy, "I have come to speak with you. Your family grieves for you. Your granddaughter will not eat, and she wants me to bring you back to her. Ivern and Minky won't leave the house and say that the Nine-Night cannot begin."

"Cuffy," replied Grandmother. "You know I can't return to the land of the living."

"Yes, but your family won't allow your spirit to be released. What will happen when the ancestors come, and you are still attached to earthly pleasures? What then?"

Grandmother looked sad, probably for the first time in her life. Then she said, "Cuffy, you can't stay any longer, or you won't be able to return. Go tell my family that I am doing well. But the Nine-Night must begin to allow me to see the faces of all the people I knew, to drink and eat spirit food, to sing and dance."

"But what if they do not believe me?" Cuffy asked.

Grandmother leaned toward Cuffy and whispered something in his ear. Then, reaching into her pocket, she placed an object into the palm of Cuffy's hand. "Give this to my sweet Kwanza and tell her what I told you."

Cuffy turned and began to walk the same route he had taken to get there, all the while beating his drum. He walked and walked and walked.

The Moon had faded in the sky and day-clean soon came. Some children were

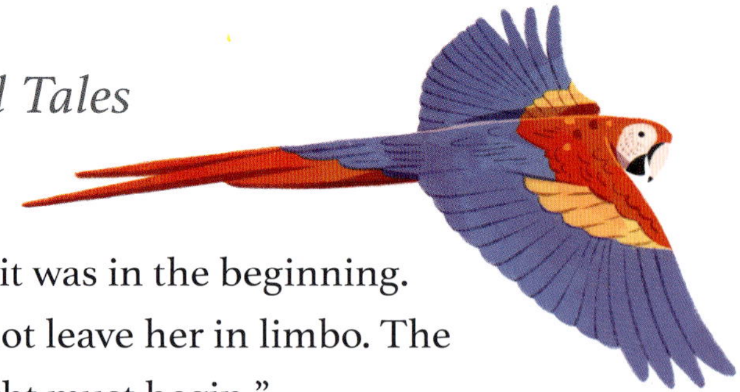

taking their early morning sea bath when they saw the water bubbling and frothing. They ran back to the beach, afraid. Then a head appeared from beneath the waves, then shoulders, then a torso, and finally, as stridently as Cuffy had walked into the sea, he now walked out again.

On seeing Cuffy, the children jumped around, spinning cartwheels and singing with delight, "Cuffy return, Cuffy return." They followed him through the village knocking on doors and telling people to rise up out of their beds.

Once again, Cuffy found himself knocking on Ivern and Minky's door. On the third knock, Ivern opened the door. Minky and Kwanza stood by his side. "I've been to see Grandmother," said Cuffy. "She told me to tell you that she loves you all very much, but life is for the living and you should live your life to the full."

Kwanza's eyes widened. "It's not true! You're telling me an Anansie story!" she cried.

"You don't believe me?" asked Cuffy.

Kwanza shook her head.

"Your grandmother said to tell you that when someone we love passes away, they go to the place of our ancestors, a spiritual realm where we will all meet again, as it was in the beginning. You cannot leave her in limbo. The Nine-Night must begin."

Cuffy placed an object into the palm of Kwanza's hand. Kwanza looked at the brightly colored stone that she and her grandmother had painted together. It seemed to shine even brighter than Kwanza remembered, and it was warm to touch. Kwanza looked up at her mother.

"I put that stone in Grandmother's hand myself on the day we laid her to rest!" said Kwanza.

Cuffy continued, "Your Grandmother said to tell you how she loves the colors on the stone, and that whenever you are lonely, you should hold it tight and it will give you the strength to remember the time you spent together."

*How could Cuffy know this?* thought Kwanza. Something rang true in the master drummer's voice, and as she stood there looking into his eyes, Kwanza could see a whole other world within them.

"Let the Nine-Night begin . . ." Cuffy said gently.

Kwanza slowly nodded in amazement and whispered to herself, "It's all true . . . the Nine-Night must begin."

She turned to her parents saying,

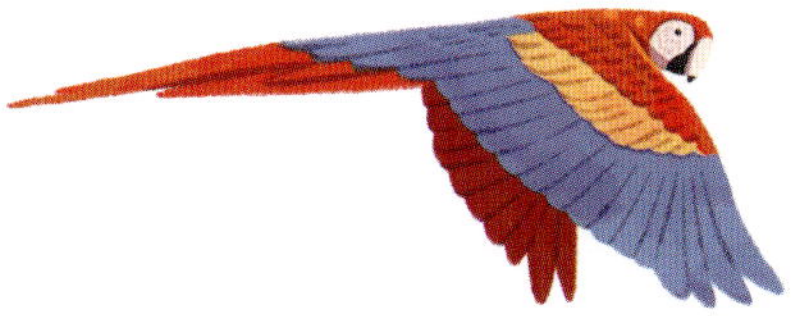



**"Let the Nine-Night begin!"**

Then, in jubilant unison, they all shouted at the top of their voices so that everyone could hear,

**"Let the Nine-Night begin!"**

Ivern walked down the wooden steps, drew some water into the calabash bowl, and poured the libation. The drummers picked up the pace, welcoming the ancestors. The Nine-Night had begun!

# Iara

## A Tale from Brazil
## Retold by Marisa Paska

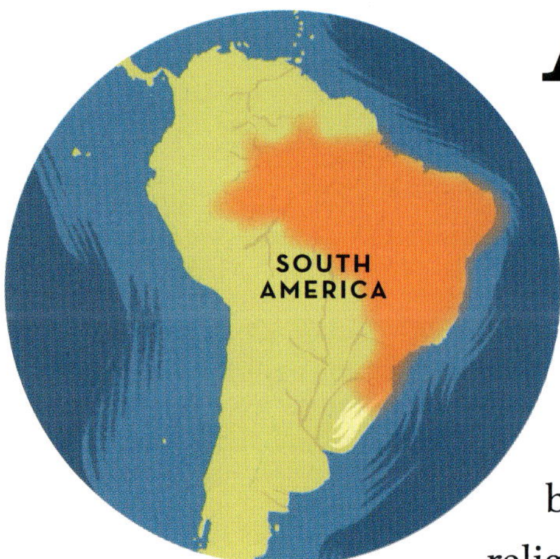


**According to Brazilian folklore, lurking in the** Tapajós River, deep in the Amazon rainforest, is a mysterious creature known as Iara. Half woman and half fish, Iara is best known for luring men to their watery deaths. It is thought that stories of a vengeful mermaid were brought over to Brazil by European colonizers in the 1600s and later blended with Indigenous Tupi tales of a ferocious river monster called Ipupiara, as well as those of Imeanjá—the beloved goddess of the sea from the Afro-Brazilian Candomblê religion. Iara would become one of the usual explanations for the disappearance of those foolhardy enough to venture alone in the jungle or stray too close to the river edge.

A long time ago, there was a young woman named Iara who lived with her tribe on the banks of the Tapajós, a mighty river running through the Amazon rainforest. Although she was young, Iara was already a skilled huntress, whose bow and arrow barely left her side.

Her prowess with a bow and arrow were second only to her striking appearance. With caramel-colored skin, long, silky hair, and piercing green eyes, Iara turned heads wherever she went.

Iara was the daughter of the *pajé*, her tribe's spiritual leader, a respected man who never missed an opportunity to tell the village how proud he was of his only daughter.

Iara's four brothers, on the other hand, were less impressed. Her beauty they could handle—it was the role of women to be beautiful, they thought. When, time after time, she bested them on the hunt, however, they began to grow jealous.

One day, they sat in a far corner of the village away from everyone else deciding what they should do about their sister.

"She must go," the four brothers agreed amongst themselves.

"She is making us look foolish," said the youngest.

"We will never gain the respect of our tribe and our father while she is here," agreed the eldest.

"We could take her into the forest, and leave her there," said another brother. "She will never find her way home."

"No," replied the eldest. "She is too skilled a tracker; she will surely return. We must kill her."

They hatched a plan to ambush Iara that very night when the tribe would be at the naming ceremony, so no one would be watching. Unfortunately for the brothers, their plan didn't remain secret. While walking back from the river, Iara saw her brothers deep in conversation. She crept silently toward them with the stealth of a jaguar tracking its prey, until she got close enough to overhear their plan.

*I must defend myself*, she thought, while quickly trying to decide what to do.

Not wanting to arouse the suspicion of her brothers, Iara prepared herself for the festival as usual. She oiled and combed her long black hair, painted her arms and face with jenipapo berries and urucum seeds, adorned herself with beads, then carefully attached a small knife to her waist and pulled her bow over her shoulder.

On her way to the celebration, she found her brothers waiting for her with malice in their eyes. Iara knew she would not be able to talk them out of their plan. When they set upon her, she acted swifty and fought valiantly, and at the end of the altercation it was the four brothers, not Iara, who lay dead on the ground.

Iara was ashamed. "I never wanted to kill them," she cried out loud, sitting on the banks of the Tapajós River, trying to wash her hands clean. Her tears dripped into the water, creating ripples that stretched across the water's surface. But it was too late. When her father

discovered the bodies of his four sons, he was enraged, making a solemn oath to his tribe's people:

"I will kill whoever did this to my sons!"

It wasn't until he found Iara, with drops of his sons' blood still smeared on her face, that he realized the error of his words. Unable to break his oath, Iara's father declared that the girl would be tied to a stone and dropped into the river to pay for the murders.

"Life pays for life," he said softly, as he watched the sentence be carried out on his only daughter.

And so it was done.

**But the spirits of the forest had seen Iara crying and had tasted her tears.**

They knew that her innocence was real and took pity on the young girl's soul.

"A life taken in self-defense does not need to be paid," they said.

As Iara drifted toward the bottom of the deepest part of the Tapajós River, resigned to her fate, the spirits of the water untied the knots that held her, and pulled Iara to the surface, saving her from the death she had been promised.

"What will I do now?" Iara asked the spirits. "I cannot return to my people. My own father condemned me to die. There is nowhere for me to go," she cried, dejectedly.

The spirits of the forest took pity on Iara yet again.

"You can stay with us," they told her.

"What do you mean?" asked Iara, but the answer was already upon her. Iara's legs began to tingle, and when she looked down, fish-like scales were sprouting on her legs, which began to lose their shape and grow together. Soon, where her legs once were, Iara had a long, green, elegant fish tail. She had been turned into a mermaid.

From that day forward, Iara lived in the river, with a human torso and a fish tail, able to breathe both underwater and in the open air. She swam the waters of the Tapajós River, her long hair glittering in the evening Sun, and rested on the rocks and sandbanks to watch the stars shoot across the sky.

Iara was happy, yet she was also sad—she loved and missed her people dearly. She mostly stayed nearby to her village to be close to them but made sure to stay out of sight if anyone came near.

One day, a group of warriors traveling from distant lands passed close to her tribe's territory carrying weapons, ready to attack. Iara became worried and called to the warriors with a sweet siren song that sang from her lips.

The men looked and saw a young woman laying on a rock in the middle of the river, whose song was more beautiful than that of the uirapuru bird. They tried

to reach her, but the current was too strong, and the men perished beneath the river's surface. Iara realized that with her song, she had saved her people.

Years passed and Iara's family lived and died. Yet Iara remained in the waters, entrancing strangers with her song in order to protect the forest and the village from outsiders. Anyone who threatened the peace would be lured into the waters, where they would drown, helplessly trying to reach the enchanting young girl who was actually a mermaid.

There were some, it is told, who survived their encounter with Iara. They returned to their villages half-crazy, only curable by a powerful *pajé*, although sometimes even the strongest magic was no match for Iara's siren song.

She became a legend, seen by few but known by all as the "Mother of the Waters," or Mãe das Águas—the deadly beauty of the Tapajós River.

Over time, however, the forest changed. There were too many dangers for Iara to keep away. Men came with chainsaws and cut down trees—the noise of the blades drowning out Iara's siren song when she tried to stop them. The villagers had to move away, and the Tapajós River began to lose its water.

The spirits of the forest were worried. Something had to be done. They decided that Iara could no longer protect the forest by staying in the river, so they gave her back her legs and told her to go into the city and find the people who used to live in the forest.

"We need them to come back to protect us again," said the spirits.

"But why people?" asked Iara "People are the ones destroying us; why would they save us?"

"They are in a war against themselves," replied the spirits. "Only people can save the forest from destruction caused by other people."

Off Iara went, away from the forest for the first time, yet on a quest to save it—a brave warrior girl with long black hair, and skin that glistened in the Sun, almost as if she had the scales of a fish.

# Pachakamaq and Pachamama

## A Tale from Peru
## Retold by Mariana Llanos

**For the Indigenous peoples of the Andes Mountains** in South America, the world is divided into three interconnected realms: Hanan Pacha—symbolized by the condor (Kuntur in the native Quechua language)—is the upper world, or the sky, where the gods reside. Kay Pacha, symbolized by the puma, is the middle world, the land, where present earthly life happens. Uku Pacha, symbolized by the serpent, or Amaru, is the underworld, associated with death but also with fertility and renewal. This story features some of the most powerful gods of Andean mythology: Pachakamaq, god creator; Pachamama, Mother Earth; Mama Killa, the Moon; and Inti, the Sun.

Long ago, two mighty brothers lived in the Hanan Pacha, the sky above. Pachakamaq was the god creator of the world. Wakon, his brother, was the god of fire and darkness. The brothers frequently played games to prove who was the strongest, the fastest, or the smartest. Every time, Pachakamaq came first, but his brother, Wakon, always insisted on a rematch.

"You're going to lose again," cautioned Pachakamaq playfully. For him those competitions were only a game. He didn't know his brother resented his power and courage, and that jealousy burned like a wildfire inside his heart.

One day, when Pachakamaq came down to Kay Pacha, the Earth, to visit his beloved creation, he met a young woman named Pachamama. Her lustrous hair reminded him of hummingbird feathers, her lively eyes of luscious flowers, but it was the compassion and generosity she showed to all living things that pulled him like a strong current. With a sweet voice, she talked to plants and animals, and they understood her! Pachakamaq's love for her flowed pure and abundant like the waters of the river. Her eyes sparkled when she looked at the handsome and caring Pachakamaq, as she too was lovestruck.

Not everyone celebrated their union. Wakon grew more bitter with each passing day as his brother's happiness blossomed on Earth in the arms of his love. And even more when they welcomed their children, the boy and girl twins called the Willkas.

Wanting to hurt his brother, Wakon turned his angry eyes toward the Earth. From the sky, he unleashed fires that turned plants into ashes and rich soil into dust. The people grew sick and begged for rain, but Wakon stopped all the clouds.

Seeing the desolation caused by his brother, Pachakamaq's anger shook the whole world. He went after his brother and with a push of his hand, he expelled Wakon from the sky.

Pachakamaq and Pachamama decided to stay on Earth to mend it. Along with their Willkas, they planted trees, cacti, and ichu grass. They bred alpacas, cuyes, and llamas. They gifted humans with different kinds of potatoes to make up for Wakon's despicable actions.

But they didn't know that evil Wakon had transformed into a monstrous feline with bulging eyes, knife-like teeth, and claws that cut like blades. He followed them around on Earth, thirsty for revenge.

One day, as Pachakamaq approached the ocean, he stepped on ground that Wakon had loosened, and fell from the cliff. He plummeted into the ocean and his human body turned into an island. His spirit returned to rule the sky, but the Earth became dark for it was he who had carried its light.

Alone with her twins, Pachamama roamed the darkened and saddened fields, searching for a safe place. They walked wearily in a cold and never-ending night. Unable to see them from his spot in the sky, Pachakamaq cried, and his tears became stars.

Suddenly, a familiar voice whispered nearby. “Come, my loves, find shelter in that cave!”

The Willkas pointed at the cave where the voice came from. “It’s Father!” they exclaimed happily. They didn’t know Wakon had faked his brother’s voice and waited for them disguised as an old man.

When Pachamama peeked her head inside the cave, she saw the old man, sitting on a big stone, stirring a pot over a fire. He smiled and gestured to them to come in.

“You must be hungry, *wawas* [babies],” he said to the children. Their stomachs churned as they nodded.

“The soup is almost ready,” said Wakon, still pretending to be the innocent old man. “But we need more water.” He handed them a clay pot. “Fill it up at the river. Don’t come back until it’s full!”

Obediently, the children parted, without noticing the tiny hole at the bottom of the pot. Alone in the cave, the monster Wakon revealed his face to a shocked Pachamama as he confessed his intentions. “Marry me!” he demanded. “Together we’ll rule the Earth!”

Trying to escape, Pachamama pushed him, but the monster Wakon sank his enormous teeth ino her, taking her life. He dragged her body and buried it outside the cave.

**Immediately, Pachamama turned into a mountain and her tears formed a snowy white poncho that adorned its peak.**

When the children came back to the cave, dragging their feet and complaining they couldn’t collect much water, they looked for their mother.

“She said you need to wait here,” Wakon lied, once again dressed as the old man. He laid down to rest, plotting cruel ways to get rid of his brother’s children.

Uneased by the old man’s beastly snoring, the children didn’t sleep. They held hands and wished for their mother to hurry.

After a while, they heard the song of the waychaw, the morning bird. They understood the bird’s language, just like their kind mother understood the language of all the living things.

“Poor Pachamama,” the bird lamented. “So generous and nurturing! That man is

a monster who took her life. Run away, for you are next! But first, tie his hair to that big stone so it takes him longer to chase after you. Hurry!"

The Willkas did as they were told and dashed from the cave. Outside waited some animals that felt compassion for the children. Añas, the skunk, urged them to climb on her back and she carried them to her den.

"Hide!" she ordered. "And don't come out for any reason."

When Wakon opened his eyes, he tried to spring, but instead, he thudded back to the ground. One by one, he snapped his hair strands loose from the stone. Sniffing the air, Wakon began to follow the faint scent of children, when Amaru, the serpent, sneaked nearby.

"Have you seen the Willkas?" asked Wakon, disguised again as an old man. "I'm worried about them!"

Amaru pointed toward the tall ichu grass, and Wakon took off running. But Amaru knew the children were nowhere near the ichu.

As Wakon searched, Puma, strolled by.

"I miss the Willkas," Wakon said sadly. "Did you see which way they went?"

Puma nodded her head toward a hill, but she knew the children were nowhere near that hill.

Almost out of breath, Wakon found Kuntur, the condor, resting on a rock.

"Those Willkas! They stole from me—help me find them!"

Kuntur extended his huge wing toward a steep mountain and Wakon followed it. But Kuntur knew the children were nowhere near the top of that mountain.

On his way to the mountain, Wakon stumbled upon Añas. By now, the scent of the Willkas had grown stronger since they had been on the animal's back. Wakon sniffed around like a wild beast.

"Where are they?" he roared, forgetting he was supposed to be a weak old man. "Tell me where to find them!"

Añas, who was a trickster, whispered,

"Those sneaky children are hiding. But if you fake their mother's voice, they'll come out. You must stand on the highest boulder to spot them quickly."

Wakon nodded, and imitating Pachamama's voice, he climbed the mountain singing: "Come my sweet *wawas*, it's time to go home. Father is waiting, don't make me wait too."

As he stepped on the boulder Añas had prepared for him, it came loose, and it rolled, rolled, rolled down the mountain, shaking the Earth with an earthquake that sank Wakon into the deepest abyss and buried his body in the Uku Pacha, the underworld.

A grateful Pachamama blessed the animals who had helped her children. Kuntur, Puma, and Amaru became revered by the people and the other animals. She rewarded Añas's bravery by allowing her to hide her babies at night like she had hidden Pachamama's children.

From his realm in the sky, Pachakamaq lowered a golden rope. The Willkas climbed toward their father. It was their time to take their places as gods for the people. The boy Willka became Inti, the Sun, and he gave light and warmth to Earth. His sister turned into Mama Killa, the Moon, and she gave a soft light to the night so people and animals could rest and grow.

Pachamama's generous spirit became one with the land and provided food and shelter to all living creatures. As the Andean Mother Earth, she watched over planting, harvesting, fertility, and weather, only asking in return that people remained grateful.

Pachakamaq and Pachamama's spirits were destined to rule different realms. But to this day, they lovingly hold hands when the sky and Earth meet on the horizon, watching over their children, the Sun and the Moon, playing a game of hide-and-seek.

# Africa

Let's journey now to Africa, through dense jungles and across sweeping savannas, where stories have been told for millennia around campfires and under starlit skies. The tales of this continent reveal a world where animals talk, spirits roam, and magic is woven into the fabric of everyday life. In the following pages, you'll meet a clever turtle who outwits her foe, learn how to stand up to bullies, and discover the importance of honoring the bond between humans and animals.

# The Spider and the Turtle

## A Tale from Nigeria
## Retold by Clifford Samuel

**There are many tricksters in West African myths and** folklore—clever, devious animals or characters that use their cunning and wit to outsmart others, usually causing mischief in their wake. In this tale, a trickster is tricked after selfishly thinking only of itself. It serves as a reminder of the value of honesty and generosity and the possibility of learning lessons from your mistakes.

Spider lived deep in the forest, where the warm, green light filtered through the leaves, and the soil was rich and dark. Spider was proud of his house, with its neat straw roof and mud brick walls, but most of all, he was proud of his garden. Today, he hummed with happiness, for it was time to gather his yams . . . and this year, they looked chunkier than ever.

"Mmm, mmm," said Spider. "These are going to be *so* delicious. Tantalizingly tasty! I can't wait."

First, Spider lit a fire. While he waited for it to burn hot enough, he stripped off the yams' rough, wrinkly, hairy skin. Then he began baking them to perfection, until they were crispy and crackling a lush golden brown.

He set the table. He laid out the yams in his best dish. He breathed in their toasty, delectable scent . . .

"At last," he sighed. "Dinnertime!"

But fate seemed to have other plans for his yams. There was a sudden:

**Knock! Knock! Knock!**

at his door. Startled, Spider hurried to answer it. There, stood his old friend, Turtle. She looked tired, and most worrying of all, both hungry and hopeful.

Now, it was the custom in Spider's land to share your meal with visitors. But Spider's greedy heart was most reluctant.

"Hello, Spider," said Turtle. "I have been out all day, busy, busy, busy, and then the aroma of those delicious yams led me to your door." Her voice sounded eager and pleading. "Would you be so kind as to share your meal with me?"

Spider could not refuse, much as he longed to. But then an idea came to him—a short, sweet idea. *Yes,* Spider thought to himself. *There's a plan. That could work . . .*

Spider carefully masked his reluctance with a wide smile.

"Please, come in, Turtle," he said. "I'd be honored to have you as my guest this evening. Take a seat—choose any chair, make yourself comfortable . . . and do help yourself."

Turtle smiled gratefully. She took a seat. Her eyes gleamed with anticipation as she reached for a yam, but before she could take it, Spider hurried to her side.

"Turtle!" he cried, in a shocked voice.

**"Don't you know better than to come to the table with dirty hands?"**

Turtle looked down at her hands and saw that they were, indeed, quite filthy. She had been walking all day and had not had a chance to wash.

"I'm so sorry," she said. "Please forgive me. I'll be as quick as I can."

With those words and with the usual pace of her nature, she left the table and walked ever so slowly down to the river, where she plunged her hands in deep.

The river water was deliciously cool as it lapped against her limbs, but Turtle's mind was only on the yams she had left behind. As soon as she was clean, she made her way back to Spider's house, moving at her natural measured stride.

"Now it's my turn to apologize," said Spider, as Turtle entered. "I've already started to eat. I didn't want these tasty yams to get cold, you see. But do join me now."

Turtle settled down and reached once more for a yam, but Spider let out an even louder yell. "Oh, Turtle! Did you not hear me before? It is not polite to come to the table with dirty hands!"

Turtle looked down and saw her clean hands were dirty all over again—for, of course, she had walked on them to get back to the house.

"How foolish of me," she said. "What was I thinking? I won't be long . . ."

So off she plodded down to the river to wash. This time, when Turtle returned, she was careful to step only on the grass, so her hands would stay clean. But by the time Turtle sat down at the table, it was empty.

Spider had finished every last mouhtful of those tasty yams.

Not so much as a slither was left.

*I see how it is*, Turtle thought to herself. She looked at Spider for a moment and then said, "Thank you for sharing your meal with me. If you ever find yourself near my house, please let me return the favor."

Then, with great dignity, she left Spider's house and went home. By now, tired, hungry Turtle was making clever, sweet plans of her own.

Days passed and Spider wondered more and more about the meal that Turtle had promised him. Every time Spider thought about it, the more delicious and mouth-watering it seemed, until at last, he couldn't bear to wait a moment longer. He set off at once, winding through the paths of the forest, down to the wide, sleepy river where Turtle lived.

Spider didn't even have to call out, for there was Turtle, warming herself on the riverbank near her home, as if she had been waiting for him all this time.

Did Turtle bear a grudge about the yams? Spider didn't think so. She looked delighted to see him.

"Welcome," said Turtle, with a warm smile. "Have you come to share my evening meal?"

"Oh yes, yes!" said Spider, growing hungrier by the minute.

"I'll just set the table for the two of us," said Turtle, and she slipped into the water.

Shortly after, she came back to the bank and said, "Your place is waiting, and the food is ready. Please join me, dear friend."

Then Turtle dived back into the water.

**Down, down, down to the riverbed she went.**

Eagerly, Spider jumped into the water to join her. But no matter how hard he swam, he kept bobbing back up to the surface.

Spider tried diving. He tried belly flops. He tried a running jump, a flying LEAP . . . but nothing worked.

*This is a DISASTER*, thought Spider. *There must be a way . . . There has to be . . .* And then he spied them—pebbles on the riverbank. "Of course!" he cried, stuffing his jacket pockets full until they hung low and heavy by his sides. Once again, he scuttled into the water.

**Down, down, down he sank, now a very satisfied spider.**

There, at the bottom, was Turtle, sitting at the table, patiently waiting. And oh! The food that was laid out! Onunu and pepper soup! Fish, prawns, crabs and crayfish, oysters, periwinkles, and èbà! Spider's mouth watered. He reached for his first bite, but before he could taste it, Turtle spoke.

"In my home," she said, mildly, "we do not wear our jackets at the table."

Spider noticed that Turtle had removed her own jacket before sitting down.

"Of course!" Spider said. "No matter."

He began to take off his jacket, but as soon as he had shrugged it off,

**he began hurtling up, up, up to the surface . . .**

the feast getting smaller and smaller before his eyes. And then, in no time at all, with a faint POP! Spider was back on the riverbank.

Suspicious now, Spider stuck his head beneath the surface. Just as he had feared, there was Turtle, down on the riverbed, a very satisfied smile on her face. Yes, she was eating the feast, and was clearly intending to eat alone.

"I outsmarted Turtle," realized Spider, dolefully, "and now she has outsmarted me."

# The Love of a Hippo

## A Tale from Kenya
## Retold by Neema Githere

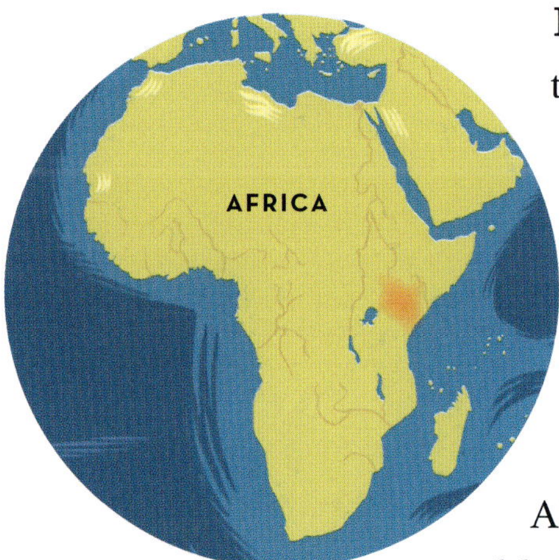


**Legend has it that long before there were roads,** the ancestors of the Abagusii people of Kenya journeyed from their home in a mystical land called Misri, wandering through formidable terrain by foot in pursuit of fertile land. Along the way, they encountered many wild animals—from leopards to baboons, zebras to hippos—that came to be the sacred guardians of each of the tribe's clans. Generations upon generations of Abagusii children have sat by the fireside, at the feet of their elders, learning these vibrant stories of their people's origins.

*"Mogano ngocha nde,"* the elders say as they begin their tales—"Story, I'm coming."

*"Mogano inchuo,"* the children respond—"Story, come."

Nyaboke was a playful child—never naughty, but always curious. Even at the age of five, the questions she asked were so intuitive that she earned herself the reputation of being an ancient spirit in a young body. Just like her mother, Monchari, Nyaboke loved the big river that flowed past their village, but she never knew why.

Monchari was a quiet and thoughtful

woman, and she often spent her afternoons by the riverbed, waiting for the hippos to emerge from the waters.

**The older Nyaboke got, the more questions she had for her mother.**

Why did her mother not have a husband, like the other women in the village? Why was the hippo so important to their clan?

One day, when Monchari and her mother were sitting by the glistening river, Nyaboke decided to ask her mother the most important question of them all . . .

"Mama, where did we come from?"

*Mogano ngocha nde. Story, I'm coming.*

"Count to seven for me, my child," Monchari responded, and Nyaboke did as her mother asked.

"Seven generations ago, a man by the name of Kintu left a mystical land called Misri because it was no longer suitable for all of us," Monchari continued. "Kintu was your father's great-great-great-great-grandfather."

Nyaboke looked down at the water in front of them, her small fingers tracing along her reflection in the deep emerald stream as she wondered what Misri must have been like.

"Mogusii, your grandfather, is the forefather of all of us Abagusii. Your father, Omache, was his youngest son.

I miss your father dearly."

Nyaboke took some time to digest what her mother said. Unlike most other children her age, Nyaboke was not hasty to respond. Patience was her friend, and this patience was a gift that made Nyaboke a delight for her mother to confide in.

*Mogano inchuo. Story, come.*

Despite all her inquisitiveness, never before had Nyaboke questioned her mother's sadness. She was so accustomed to it by now that she assumed it had always been this way. But as Nyaboke watched her mother's eyes well up, she saw for the first time that it was loss that made her mother so sad.

"I have wanted to tell you this story for some time now, Nyaboke," continued Monchari. Her voice trailed off as the sentence went on, showing a reluctance that was quite unlike the composure that Nyaboke was used to seeing from her mother. "I was very afraid the day your brother was born. That same day, I had received news that your father had been

killed in battle."

Nyaboke had heard versions of this story from her agemates—whispers about how her mother had rebelled and fled remarriage and her own homestead.

The two sat in nurturing silence for some time, giving Nyaboke's mother some time to regain her composure.

*Mogano inchuo. Story, come.*

"I knew that it would be expected of me to take a new husband, but your father was my one true love. And so that same day, I left our land with you and your brother so that I would not be made to remarry. The path was long and dangerous. Along the way, we encountered leopards and lions, and there were heavy rains."

Nyaboke gazed out to the other side of the river, where thick trees in their countless shades of green formed a dense layer of horizon. Her mother had taught her to pray to Engoro, their God, every time she felt afraid. Before her mother continued with her tale, Nyaboke had an impulse to whisper a short prayer.

"Nyaboke, the journey was not an easy one. The waters had grown treacherous, destroying everything in our path, and we almost drowned in the flood. Just when I thought we were not going to survive, a hippo emerged from beneath the water and carried us to safety. That is why our clan reveres them," Monchari explained.

Almost like clockwork, the water in front of them began to bubble. A hippo was near. Its ears were the first to emerge from the river, followed by its bulging eyes—a sight grotesque to many, but beloved by Monchari. The tears Nyaboke's mother had tried to suppress returned as a stream and trailed down her high cheekbones as her face curled up into a warm, wide smile.

"Come!" Monchari exclaimed, more youthful in her zeal than Nyaboke had seen for some time, as she grabbed her daughter's hand and led her to the water.

"Oh Engoro!" Monchari exhaled with glee, turning toward her daughter. "I have taught you to pray because Engoro answered my own prayers through this creature."

The hippo thrust its mouth open, as though it were about to laugh. Then, to Nyaboke's amazement, the creature spoke:

---

"Nyaboke, you must never fear me."

---

"For so long as you vow to respect my kind, I will protect all the people in your clan. You will be told I am ugly. You will be told that I am dangerous, but it was I who carried you through the storms that threatened to swallow you."

Many years later, when Nyaboke's granddaughter asked why their clan did not fear hippos, Nyaboke simply replied: "Do not ask me about fear, my child—ask me how I came to know about love. We must never harm those who have protected us the way that the hippopotamus protected me and my mother. This is why it is forbidden for all those in our clan to hunt or kill a hippo."

# Why the Owl Flies at Night

## A Tale from Zimbabwe
## Retold by Blessing Musariri

**Once upon a very long time ago in the forests** of Dzimbamabwe, the beasts of the Earth and the birds of the air could talk. Their stories now live among us as tales told by our parents and their parents right back to the beginning of humankind. This is the story of why Zizi, the owl, flies at night.

One fateful morning in the great forest of Dzimbamabwe, the birds of the air gathered in and around a spreading msasa tree that stood in the middle of a clearing. Green moss clung to its gray and black bark like tufts of beard and swayed in the wind. Zizi and his two bodyguards, Bat Hawk One and Bat Hawk Two, came down with a great beating of wings and fluffing of feathers to perch on the topmost branch of the big tree. Zizi was feared by all the other birds because of the scary horns on either side of his head which he was always threatening to use if he didn't get his way, so when he called a meeting, they all attended whether they wanted to or not.

"What does Zizi want now?" whispered Nhengure, the fork-tailed drongo, to Hadada Ibis. She was fed up of Zizi's commands.

"Listen here," said Zizi. "I shall no

longer fly about hunting for food, because I have much more important things to do!"

"Such as what?" called out Hadada Ibis.

"Such as making a list of who shall be the first to experience the sharpness of my horns. Do you see them?"

Zizi swooped down ferociously among the birds, making the leaves tremble and the moss release its hold and fall to the forest floor. He ruffled the feathers of the birds he flew past, shoving roughly, and while Bat Hawks One and Two beat their wings menacingly about the birds' heads, Zizi pecked them sneakily with his beak.

The birds scattered, crying out each time Zizi pecked them.

"Ouch!" cried Mousebird in pain and fear. "He really does have horns and they are sharp."

"Ha!" said Zizi in satisfaction as he returned to his perch. "You'd better do as I say, or it will be even worse for you."

The birds grumbled among themselves because there had been a drought and food was hard to find. But none of them wanted another demonstration of Zizi's horns so they had to do what he said.

Nhengure, a wise and thoughtful bird, was not so sure. She knew that Zizi was not the strongest, biggest, or smartest bird, but he was definitely the meanest. She suspected Zizi was taking advantage of all of them and knew he needed to be stopped before the other birds became used to doing what Zizi commanded. She had flown up high during the commotion and tried to see exactly how Zizi's horns worked, but there had been too much noise and movement.

Nhengure realized she needed to be smart because Zizi's two tough bodyguards, Bat Hawk One and Bat Hawk Two, only left his side at dusk to hunt, and even then, they only went one at a time. Nhengure could not count on the courage of the other birds as they had become convinced that Zizi would use his dangerous horns on them. So, she thought and watched and waited.

As the days went by, the birds would bring any food they found to Zizi before feeding themselves with whatever was left. Bat Hawks One and Two would fly around menacingly, pushing all the birds away so Zizi could pick the best food for himself. Only when he was satisfied could the other birds eat. Zizi became fat while all the other birds became thin.

One day, little Sandgrouse, faint with hunger, fell straight down from the sky into the long grass below.

"This is hard work," he complained. "We fly for hours and hours, farther and farther, and Zizi eats more and more, while we grow weak with hunger."

"This cannot go on," said Guineafowl. "If I could fly as high as the rest of you, I would challenge Zizi and knock him off his pedestal. I'm big enough."

The other birds didn't take Guineafowl seriously. They knew she was only saying that because there was no way she could fly as high as Zizi perched, so she would never have to prove that she was truly that brave.

"I can fly as high," said Marabou Stork, "but I'm not as quick, because I'm even bigger than Guineafowl."

"No," said Nhengure. "Speed and size are all every well, but we must use cunning as we also have to deal with Bat Hawk One and Bat Hawk Two. I have been watching Zizi very closely when he comes down to pick and choose his food. I have a suspicion that he has been lying to us, and we must expose him once and for all. Gather round, I have a plan."

Nhengure was not only thoughtful and wise, but she and her fellow fork-tailed drongos could also imitate the calls of other birds, and this was going to be very important for what they needed to do.

The next day at dusk, all the birds took their positions in and around the big msasa tree in the forest clearing. Some, like Guineafowl and Quail, hid in the long grass so that Zizi and his guards wouldn't get suspicious. Bat Hawk One left to do his hunting while Bat Hawk Two stayed behind to guard Zizi, who was taking a nap. Suddenly, Bat Hawk Two cocked his head to listen.

"Number Two, Number Two, I need help! Come right away! Help me!" It was Nhengure's cousin in the nearby valley imitating Bat Hawk One's alarm call.

Bat Hawk Two looked at Zizi, who was fast asleep, dreaming, his chin tucked into his feathers. He'd be back before Zizi even knew he'd gone.

As soon as he left, Marabou and his friend swooped down on either side of

Zizi, grabbed him, and brought him down to the clearing where Guineafowl, Quail, and some wading birds were waiting. Mousebird, Sandgrouse, and the other small birds circled the air just above, and Nhengure landed on Zizi's head, rifling through Zizi's "horns" with her claws.

"What is happening?" Zizi cried out,

thinking he was having a nightmare.

He was still in between waking and sleeping. “Get off me!” he cried. He tried to free himself, but Marabou Stork pinned him down.

“Ha! Look everyone!” Nhengure called out. “Zizi has no horns. These are simply feathers shaped like horns. He can’t hurt anyone with them.”

All the birds were atwitter with outrage.

“You’re just like all of us,” called Hadada Ibis. “There’s nothing fearsome about you at all.”

“No horns! No horns!” cried Go-Away Bird, “No horns!”

Guineafowl kicked up sand and Zizi shielded his eyes with his wings. All the birds flapped and tweeted furiously around Zizi. Zizi felt afraid of what they would do to him. So, with one mighty push, he took off into the descending darkness. From that day on, he was never seen again, except at night, when all the birds from the forest clearing were sleeping.

---

**And that is why Zizi—and all owls—fly at night.**

---

# Europe

With its rich tapestry of cultures and people, Europe has a long tradition of folktales and legends. Many of these stories take place deep within the ancient forests that once covered the land and tell of a magical past inhabited by fairies, trolls, witches, and fire-breathing dragons. Here, you'll meet a princess who takes a walk on the wild side by transforming into a bear, a kind-hearted heroine who tries to end a war with the help of a tiny bird, and a woodland elf that grants wishes.

# The Bear Princess

## A Tale from England
## Retold by Mary Sebag-Montefiore

**This story is an English folktale, remembering** the time, over a thousand years ago, when bears still lived in the thick forests that once cloaked the land. It is an interesting tale, as it has a female hero who is the driving force of the story, and who also gets to perform her own magic.

Once there was a king who loved his only child—a daughter—so much that he feared something dreadful would happen to her if she left the palace, so he shut her up in a tower. The princess loved her father, but felt like a prisoner. She'd gaze out of the windows at the sweeping skies and wish she could be free. She had nothing to do, except help with the housework, and she grew very good at it. But, of course, it wasn't enough.

"I'm sad," she'd tell her nurse.

"Wait till the time is right, my honey," her nurse would reply, "and then we'll see."

The nurse was really a witch, though no one knew this. When the princess reached adulthood the nurse said, "Your father loves you very much. Whatever you want, he'll give you. Ask him for a wheelbarrow and his bearskin coat, then bring them to me."

The princess was surprised, and so was the king, at this strange request.

"Why do you want them?" he asked.

"You never let me leave the house—at least grant me this," she begged, knowing that he would. And he did.

The princess brought the items to her nurse, who threaded her darning needle with yarn. This she twisted and turned until it lengthened and thickened into a magic wand made of hawthorn.

"Now put on the bearskin coat," said the nurse.

The princess obeyed, her eyes bright with excitement, especially when the nurse touched her with the wand. Immediately, she was disguised as a bear. No one could tell that a human girl breathed beneath the hide of a hairy, scary bear.

"Climb into the wheelbarrow," said the nurse, and as the princess clambered in, the nurse tapped it with the magic hawthorn. "This will make the wheelbarrow move by itself," she added. "Wherever you tap the wheelbarrow, just once, it will take you in that direction. And whenever you need help, you must tap it twice and the wheelbarrow will solve your predicament. You and the wheelbarrow will be invisible until you leave the palace gates. Now off you go."

She opened the door and tucked the wand safe in the princess's paw. The princess couldn't see herself or her wheelbarrow, but she wasn't afraid. She trusted her nurse, so she thanked her, shot out, and drove away.

Once she was beyond the palace gates, she was visible again; a brown bear racing in a rackety, rolling wheelbarrow.

**For the first time ever, she felt as free as the wild wind.**

As she tapped the wheelbarrow to take her to the forest, her bear curls unfurled all over her, echoing her release.

**"I LOVE it!" she exclaimed, as she whizzed down the wild forest tracks.**

Trees, sunshine, wild roses . . . oh, the scents! And birdsong . . . red squirrels . . . deer . . .

Suddenly, she heard the blasts of a hunting horn, and before she could hide, she was surrounded by a pack of snarling dogs, led by a prince on horseback.

"Call off your dogs at once!" she cried.

The prince quieted the pack, so amazed to hear the bear speak that he asked, "Will you come home with me? My mother would like to meet a talking bear."

"Certainly," replied the princess.

*This is my chance to explore the world,* she thought, tapping her wheelbarrow to follow him, which amazed the prince even more.

His mother was equally surprised, but she, and everyone in the palace, was enchanted by the bear's conversation, charm, and skill at housework.

Months passed. Seasons turned. And the bear princess never told anyone who she really was. Whenever she wanted, she would take off in her wheelbarrow to the forest, reveling in her freedom, but she always came back, because she had fallen in love with the prince.

One day, lying under the table, her favorite place, the bear princess heard the prince was going to a ball that same evening on the other side of the forest.

"Take me too!" she cried, emerging from under the table. "I'd love to dance!"

**"Don't be ridiculous," said the prince. "A bear can't go to a ball."**

When he left, the bear princess asked if she could follow the prince—just to watch from a distance, and the queen, sorry for her, agreed.

The bear ran to her wheelbarrow.

"Now is my predicament! Please help me," she pleaded quietly, tapping the wheelbarrow twice with her magic wand. Instantly, to her delight, the wheelbarrow became a fine carriage drawn by four gray mares.

"This is no time to be a bear," she decided, tapping the wheelbarrow twice more. At once, the bearskin fell away from her, and she was herself again, dressed in a ballgown woven from moonbeams.

At the ball, she danced with the prince who, from the moment their fingers touched, wished to dance with no one else.

"Have we met before?" he asked, but she only answered with a secret smile. As the evening unfolded, her kindness delighted him, her conversation enthralled him, while her charm spread over him, as endearing and sparkling as the Sun.

Before the ball was over, she hastened away so as to be home before him. The prince leapt on his horse and cantered after her, but a great mist crept over the forest, and she was lost to sight.

When she was a bear again, lying in her usual place under the table, she heard the prince return and tell his mother all about her.

"I must see her again," he kept saying.

In those days, balls lasted for many days. On the second night, the prince was determined to go, hoping to see the girl he had danced with.

And sure enough, there she was, even more radiant than the night before, for this time her dress was woven out of sunbeams. All evening the prince danced with her, and knew he was in love. He wanted to tell her, but she left just before the last notes of music died away. As he followed her outside, jumping onto his fastest stallion, a great storm broke. Lightning zigzagged the sky.

When he arrived home, soaking wet and in despair, the prince told his mother, "I fear I will never see her again." Upon hearing this, the bear princess, curled under the table, smiled a secret smile.

On the third night of the ball, the bear princess arrived in a coach drawn by dappled grays in a dress of starlight, looking so dazzling that all eyes centered on her.

Before the dancing began, the prince placed a golden ring with a glittering stone on the princess's finger. She looked at him with joy, and together they spun around the room until the music slowed, and then she fled.

The prince tried to follow her to her carriage, but as soon as he was at the door, she had disappeared. His ring, however, was safely under her tongue.

A great wind blew him back as he tried to find her, and when he finally came home, his heart heavy with sadness, the bear princess said, "I will make you feel better. Let me make you a bowl of hot soup."

Too desolate to reply, the prince

slumped at the table, his head in his hands.

The bear princess prepared the soup, slipping her ring into the broth. The prince drank it slowly and languidly, thinking about the lost damsel of the dance. When he got to the bottom of the bowl, he was astonished to see the ring.

"How did it get there?" he asked.

"My prince, that ring traveled by starlight drawn by four dappled gray horses that outran a mighty wind."

The prince looked into her eyes and he knew.

"Take off that skin, and reveal the mystery hidden beneath it," he said.

The bearskin fell off and there she stood. He led her to his mother, who was delighted that her son should have so good a wife.

The next ball was their wedding. The bear princess invited her father, who was sorry now that he'd locked her up, and her old nurse, who promised to look after their babies one day.

As for the bear princess . . . she kept the hawthorn wand. Sometimes she would change back into a bear and run to the forest, loving its wildness. The prince made a law that no one in his kingdom would ever hunt a bear again, so she always felt safe to stop and drink in the beauty and freedom of the forest.

# Branwen

## A Tale from Wales
## Retold by Frances Evans

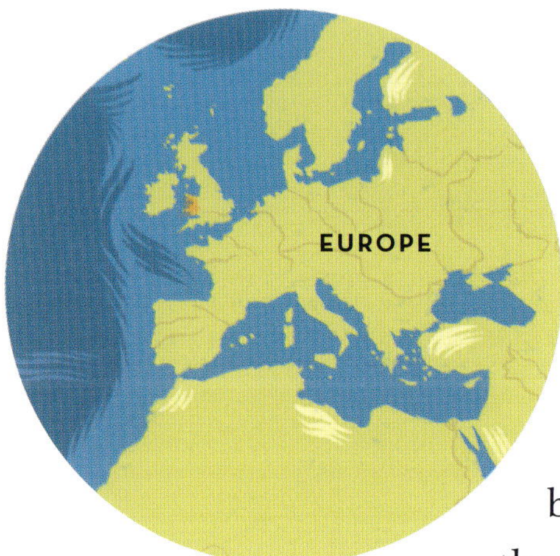


**Wales, a small country on the west coast of** Britain, is a land rich in magic and storytelling. This tale comes from a very old collection of Welsh stories known as The Mabinogion, which takes us back to a time when sorcerers wandered Wales's forests, and brave heroes undertook seemingly impossible quests. It begins not in Wales but in Ireland, where we meet a young woman imprisoned in the kitchens of a castle . . .

Branwen stood on tiptoe so she could reach the kitchen's high window. Each morning before she started her work, scrubbing the castle's floors and cleaning crusty pots, and every night before she curled up to sleep among the sacks of grain, the girl would peer through the narrow window that looked over the Irish Sea.

On a clear day, far across the gray waters, Branwen could just make out the isle of Anglesey and the Welsh mountains beyond it. Sometimes, Branwen thought she could see bursts of fire over the peaks, for dragons still roamed Wales in those days.

Today, a fog surrounded the castle and Branwen could barely make out the beach below. She was about to turn away when she heard a faint "Cheep!"

Huddled on the window ledge was a

tiny, shivering bird—a baby starling, not long out of its nest.

"Poor thing," whispered Branwen. She cupped her hand gently under the chick and brought it inside.

With Branwen's care, the little chick recovered. Soon, it lost its baby feathers and grew adult ones. As Branwen watched the bird fly around the kitchen one morning, she noticed its wings shimmering green and purple in the sunlight. Landing on her shoulder, the starling nibbled her ear gently.

Branwen wasn't sure if it was because she was so lonely, but she felt the bird understood her—and she had an idea.

"Starling!" said Branwen, "You are my only friend in this castle. I want to tell you how I came to be here. I am Branwen, Princess of Wales. My brother, Brân, and I ruled our country together until Matholwch, the king of Ireland, came to ask for my hand in marriage. I accepted because I believed it would create peace between our peoples.

"I thought that we would work together to care for Ireland. But I soon realized that Matholwch had no interest in sharing power. He didn't like it when I spoke my mind, and so he banished me to these kitchens. For three years, I have been imprisoned here. Matholwch has forbidden any boat to sail to Wales, so my brother won't find out how badly I am being treated.

"Now, starling," said Branwen. "I cannot leave these walls, but you can. Will you fly to Wales and take a message to my brother?"

The bird had been shown such kindness by the princess, it was only too happy to help. Branwen cut a scrap of cloth from her apron and wrote a message to her brother with a piece of charcoal from the fire. Considering the starling's long journey, she tied the note to the bird's wing, so it could still use its feet to rest.

Branwen took the bird to the window overlooking the sea.

"You should find my brother at his castle in Harlech. If you fly toward the mountains, you won't be able to miss it. It's also not hard to miss my brother. I forgot to mention—he's a giant!"

With that, the girl released the bird and the starling flapped away across the sea.

A few days later, the giant Brân was sitting on a hill in the shadow of the great moutain of Yr Wyddfa, when he felt something nibbling his ear—a starling! The bird ruffled its feathers so Brân could see the note fastened to its wing.

"Hello, little bird," said Brân in his deep, gentle voice. "What do you have there?"

Brân's hands were too big to undo the dainty knot, so he took the bird back to his castle, where his courtiers freed Branwen's letter.

Brân read it with a heavy heart. The giant had always valued his sister's wisdom and kind nature. The thought of her being imprisoned was unbearable.

Without delay, he sent horsemen across Wales to let the country know of Branwen's fate. The princess was much loved by the people of Wales and, as the news spread, men and women came from far and wide—some from the remote mountain farms of the north, others from

the rolling valleys of the south. Soon, Brân had mustered an army and was ready to set sail for Ireland.

No boat was large enough to carry Brân, but he was used to this. As the ships raised their anchors, the giant strode across the sand dunes in front of Harlech castle, past the windblown cliffs, and waded into the ocean.

Back in Ireland, a pig farmer was gazing out to sea when he saw a strange sight. A forest was moving across the waves and, in its center was a mountain. The farmer rubbed his eyes. Yes—there was a mountain with two caves in the middle and two lakes on either side. He rushed to the castle to tell King Matholwch.

"Fetch Branwen," said Matholwch. "No doubt this is some Welsh magic."

Branwen was brought up from the kitchens for the first time in years to join the king and his men on the battlements.

"That is not a forest," she said. "Those are the masts of hundreds of Welsh ships. I sent a message to my brother and he is coming to free me. That 'mountain' is his nose. Where the water gets deep, he puts his head back to breathe. Those caves are his nostrils, and the lakes are his eyes."

Matholwch and his men were terrified. They were not prepared for any sort of battle, let alone one involving a giant! It was decided that the safest thing to do would be to abandon the castle and

retreat inland, taking Branwen with them. If they could cross the River Liffey and destroy the bridge that ran over it, that would buy them some time. Without delay, they put their plan into action.

Meanwhile, the Welsh ships had landed in Ireland. As he waited for his men to disembark, Brân emptied his boots of water and shook seaweed from his hair.

It didn't take Brân and his troops long to reach the river. The bridge that had stood across it had been set on fire by Matholwch's men, and what remained was still smoking. The river was flowing fast beneath it.

"What shall we do without a bridge, my lord?" asked one of Brân's soldiers.

**"He who is leader," said Brân, "let him be a bridge."**

Carefully, the giant lay down across the dangerous waters, resting his arms on one side of the river and his feet on the other.

"Walk across me," he called out to his soldiers. "It is perfectly safe."

One by one, the soldiers climbed up Brân's great boots and trod gently along his body. It took several hours for all the men, women, and horses to get across, but the mighty Brân held strong. Eventually,

everyone had reached the other side of the river.

Matholwch and his army saw they were outnumbered, but they turned to face the Welsh soldiers. Each side raised their swords high, preparing to attack . . .

## "Stop!" cried a small voice at Brân's feet.

Brân squinted down—and saw his sister.

"Brân, I knew you'd come!" called Branwen. "But I don't want anyone to be killed. I want there to be peace between our countries."

Brân scratched his head. He'd had a long day and had been looking forward to teaching Matholwch a lesson. But he had always listened to his sister's advice and seeing her safe was the most important thing. He agreed to stop the fighting.

The next day, Branwen, Brân, and their army made their way back to Wales. Branwen was overjoyed to see the blue mountains get closer and closer.

"Where would you like to go, sister?" asked Brân, who was walking beside her boat.

"Can you take me to Anglesey?" asked Branwen. "I could just see its cliffs from Ireland and it gave me hope that I'd return to Wales one day. I'd like to make my home there."

Willingly, Brân tugged his sister's ship in the direction of Anglesey.

As Branwen was about to set foot on the island, a bird landed on her shoulder —her starling.

**"Thank you, friend," said Branwen. "Now, go and be free like me."**

The starling nibbled her ear one last time. Then Branwen watched as the bird flew off into the setting sun, until it was just a speck in the sky over the mountain of Yr Wyddfa.

# The Seven Wishes

## A Tale from Sweden
## Retold by Anika Hussain

**The forests of Sweden, with their branching pine** trees and mossy trails that lead to the unknown, have long been a home to all kinds of magical creatures. It is where people stumble across trolls, witches, fairies, or, if you're anything like young Olle Nilsson, a magical elf. It is also where people can begin the journey to finding themselves.

If you were ever to take a walk through Tiveden forest in Sweden, it would be impossible to miss Olle Nilsson. You would recognize him by his hair, which is often unbrushed and stiff, and his cheeks, which are always tinged with red.

One day, Olle lay on the forest floor, his knapsack beside him, looking up at the trees. He had been on the ground for a while and made no attempt to get up. You see, Olle was lazy. When he fell, he would wait for someone to help him up. When he felt a task was too difficult, he would pass it on to someone else. And when he did attempt a task, he wouldn't think it through and do it correctly. But most of all, despite relying on the help of other people, he wouldn't help others himself.

But that was about to change. Lying on the pine needle carpet, he turned his head and saw a snake not too far away.

Olle was frozen in fear until he saw that the snake wasn't interested in him but was looking at something else: a frog. Seemingly unaware of the danger it was in, the frog moved toward the snake. Soon, it was only a few inches away from the snake's mouth. Olle wondered why it was so stupid.

Angrily, Olle got up and grabbed a nearby stick.

"You silly little frog!" he shouted as he poked the frog to the side.

The snake slithered away into the forest, and the frog hopped toward Olle, letting out a short croak. Then, right in front of Olle's eyes, it transformed into an elf with eyes as deep as the ocean, cheeks as rosy as a winter apple, and hair as golden as the Sun. Olle was so surprised, he couldn't speak.

"Thank you, my friend!" said the elf, her voice soft. "You are probably wondering how I have turned from a frog to an elf."

Olle nodded.

"Well, just yesterday, I did something terribly bad. I too saw a frog that was being hunted by a snake, but, unlike you, I did not help it, I simply laughed. Fortunately, the frog escaped and returned to its true form, a prince. However, since I hadn't helped him, the prince turned me into a frog. If it hadn't been for you, I would have been eaten."

Olle still couldn't find the words to respond to the elf.

"You have done a great deed, and for that I must reward you. I will grant you seven wishes, anything you could ever want. But, please, beware—do not wish for anything foolish. If you do, you will instantly regret it. Until then . . . I bid you farewell!"

And with that, the elf soared away through the forest.

Olle stood there with his jaw hanging. He had seven wishes, and he could wish for anything. What did he want? He scratched his head in thought for a while until he realized exactly what he wanted.

"I wish that this knapsack would take me home! It is far too heavy, and I can't possibly carry it by myself."

As soon as the words had left Olle's mouth, the knapsack began to float. Olle quickly grabbed hold of it and soon found himself whizzing through the forest, leaves and stones passing by him in a blur and his face scraped by shrubs and branches. As he neared his cottage, he was suddenly flung off the knapsack so hard that he was thrown against the front door, earning himself a painful bump on his forehead.

"What happened to you, Olle?" his mother asked when she heard the noise outside.

But Olle was in so much pain from the bump to his forehead that he wasn't able to speak and tell his mother all about the elf he had met.

"Oh dear, you've really hurt yourself, haven't you? Let me get you something to eat!"

Olle's mother returned with his favorite treat: caramel-covered almonds. As he licked his hands clean of the sweet coating, he said out loud, "Oh, how I wish I had a whole bowl full of these almonds!"

The bowl of almonds appeared in front of him within seconds and Olle wasted no time in indulging again in the sweetly covered nuts. But Ollie ate the nuts so quickly that he gave himself a stomachache, and for the rest of the day, he lay in bed, groaning in pain.

Later that day, Olle was asked by his mother to clean out their small vegetable patch. Reluctantly, Olle trudged outside, but instead of carrying out the task, he simply laid down and looked up at the magnificent cherry tree above him. Olle desperately wanted to eat the cherries on the highest branch, which he could see were the reddest of them all. Thoughtlessly, he said out loud,

"Oh, how I wish I was in that tree!"

And within seconds, he was whisked up to the top of the tree, his legs hanging on one of the branches.

But Olle had made a grave mistake. He had left the gate to the garden open, and a pig had made its way to the tree to scratch its body against it. The tree began to sway, forcing Olle to cling to a branch as he was thrown back and forth. Unfortunately, he lost his grip, and he fell to the ground with such a bump that his hand was broken, his nose swollen, and there were scratches all over his face.

You'd think that after a third silly wish Olle would stop to think before wasting another one, but he had yet to learn his lesson. A few days later, as Olle headed down to the village, he saw a cyclist.

"Oh, I do wish I had a bicycle so I, too, can travel far and wide!"

And just like that, Olle was on a bicycle. But it turned out to be another foolish wish for Olle did not know how to brake. Instead, he kept cycling up and down roads, and over crops and flower beds, shouting at people and animals alike to get out of his way.

"Help me!" he yelled.

The people of the town had watched in annoyance as Olle had destroyed their crops. Now, they approached cautiously. Once they were close enough, one person put a stick through the wheel of Olle's bicycle, causing him to tumble forward and onto the ground.

Olle was so angry at the bicycle that he used his fifth wish: "I wish this stupid bicycle would break into a hundred pieces!"

Immediately, the bicycle broke into pieces in front of his eyes.

"How could you do this?" one of the townspeople asked Olle. "Don't you understand the damage you have caused?"

"You are so silly and thoughtless," said another. "If only you took a moment to think through your actions."

Olle was so ashamed that he lowered his head. He limped his way back home, mulling over what the townspeople had said. Was it true that he always got into trouble because he didn't think things through?

"I have used nearly all my wishes," he realized. "I must choose my next one carefully."

Then he had an idea. He wanted to understand himself better and he knew that you could learn lots of things by reading, something he had never done before because he was only interested in doing other things like throwing sticks. So Olle said, "I wish I could read."

Now, this was a sensible wish, and sensible wishes, unlike silly ones, are granted over time rather than immediately. But eventually, Olle was able to read. With his desire to read came a desire to learn, and he didn't give up, even when things became difficult.

Olle came to understand how foolish he had been for wasting his wishes. He had selfishly asked for things that only benefited him. Olle learned, finally, not to be lazy and that helping yourself is also about helping others.

One day, when Olle was walking through the forest again, he stumbled upon the elf.

"You have used six wishes, but out of those, only one was wise," the elf said. "Now you have one left and I do hope that it is a good one, as after that I will not be able to help you anymore."

Olle smiled. This time, he knew what he truly longed for. "I wish to become a good and useful person."

The elf beamed at him. "That's the best thing you have ever wished for. And while I will grant you this, you can only truly become a good and useful person through hard work. Keep working on yourself and for others, and it will happen. With that, I bid you farewell!"

Olle's final wish did come true. He worked hard, trying his best not only for himself but for those around him. And that, is how lazy, silly Olle realized the value of helping others.

# Asia

Prepare to enter the captivating realm of Asian folklore, where mighty dragons soar through the sky and magical beings lurk on misty mountaintops. From the epic legends of ancient China to enchanting fables of India, these tales are filled with wisdom and humor, and offer lessons in kindness, fairness, and free will. In this chapter, you will discover a parrot that longs for freedom, a kindhearted hero who tries to outwit a tyrannical king, a brave little bee, and a marvelous magical dragon boat.

# The Merchant and the Parrot

## A Tale from Ancient Persia
## Retold by Zara Sekhavati

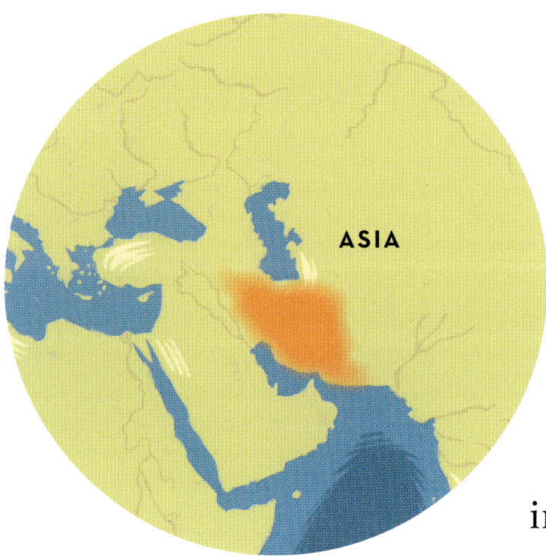


**The Silk Road was a collection of trade routes that** linked Asia and Europe from the second century BCE until the mid-fifteenth century CE. Many years ago, in the land of Persia, which was part of the Silk Road, there lived a merchant named Azad. He loved to travel and collect beautiful treasures along the way to trade. As we find out in this story, Azad's clever parrot may be his most impressive find of all.

Azad reveled in finding new discoveries from around the world. He traveled up and down the Silk Road finding amazing things to sell back home. He visited Pakistan, where he discovered intricately carved wooden boxes. He traveled to India, where he came across delicate silk.

But Azad soon discovered that his favorite things were birds. In fact, he liked them so much, he kept them for himself rather than selling them. His favorites included a laughing dove from Turkmenistan and a greater flamingo from Türkiye. Both had beautiful feathers and they could fly high into the sky. But there was one bird he was particularly fond of—the parrot he'd found in China.

The parrot was a bold and clever bird that had learned how to talk. He enjoyed chattering throughout the day and the merchant loved to listen. But Azad kept the parrot in a cage so that he couldn't fly away.

Soon, Azad had plans to travel to China again to trade. Before leaving, he spoke to his parrot.

**"I would like to bring you back a present from China," he said.**

"What would you like? What will make you happy?"

The parrot had a long think about his answer, and then replied, "When you visit China, please give a big hello to my parrot friends who live there. Please ask them if they have any advice that would make me happy. I miss my friends, which makes me feel sad."

Azad nodded and agreed to do as the parrot had asked. He said farewell to his collection of birds and gave the parrot a big wave. He then left Persia to travel to China, alongside his donkeys, which would carry the goods he wanted to trade.

After a while, Azad had sold everything he had taken to China—all the soft carpets, fancy teapots, and fragrant spices—which made him very happy. Azad had also bought plenty of goods from China to sell later in Persia. His donkeys carried many items, from fine jewelry to dazzling fabric, all the way back home on their backs.

However, Azad didn't forget his promise to his parrot. Before returning to Persia, he went deep into the Chinese jungle to find his parrot's beloved friends. He walked past tall trees and spotted monkeys and big bears. Finally, he found

his parrot's friends perched on a tree branch, flapping their wings and looking out into the bright sky. The parrots were wild and free to fly away whenever they wished. There was not a cage in sight.

"Hello, dear parrots," Azad said. "My parrot back in Persia has a message for you. He says that he misses you all dearly." The parrots looked sad; it was clear that they missed their friend too. Azad continued, "Do you have any advice for him that will make him happy?"

---

**The parrots chatted amongst themselves.**

---

Azad couldn't hear what they were saying. Then there was total silence. Suddenly, one of the parrots went very still and dropped down from the tall tree. Azad was upset, thinking the parrot had died, and he hurried back out of the jungle. The merchant was very sad, thinking he was the cause of the parrot's death. He was unsure whether to tell his parrot back in Persia what had happened, as he thought it would make the bird very upset too.

When Azad returned to Persia, he unpacked all the goods he had bought in China from the donkeys' backs. But he didn't say a word to the parrot.

The parrot later asked him, "Sir Azad, did you speak to my friends in the jungle? What did they say to you? Did they have any advice for me?"

Azad replied truthfully. "Your parrot friends did not say anything to me. They didn't give you any advice."

The parrot turned his head. Azad continued with a tear in his eye, "But one parrot dropped out of a tree suddenly and fell to the floor and died."

Azad's parrot did not say anything back to his owner. He was quiet and still. Then, all of a sudden, the exact thing that had happened in China happened again in Persia—the parrot dropped to the floor of his cage.

*Oh, this is terrible! I've caused the death of another bird*, thought Azad. *My parrot has died because of the huge sadness I caused in his life.*

Azad opened the door of the cage slowly; tears were rolling down his face. He lifted the parrot out of the cage gently and held the bird in his arms. Azad cried; he was so sad that his parrot had died.

Full of guilt and unhappiness, Azad decided to find a place for his dear parrot to rest peacefully. He picked a quiet spot under a big blossoming tree near his home, and carried the parrot there in his arms.

As Azad kneeled down and prepared to lay the bird upon the ground, he felt movement. The parrot began to wriggle around in his arms. Azad was stunned.

**What was happening? Was the parrot alive?**

The parrot stretched his big bright wings—the colors were vibrant and

beautiful. Azad had never seen such pretty feathers before. The parrot looked at his wide wings, smiled, and flew up, up, and away high into the air, far away from Azad's hold.

**"You're alive!" Azad cheered with joy, clapping his hands with happiness. "How wonderful!"**

The parrot flew up to the top of a nearby tree. He perched on one of the branches, looking down at Azad.

"This is the most alive I have ever been in my life, Sir Azad! You kept me in a cage for a very long time, but now look at me—I spread my wings and I am finally free! Thank you for this freedom—my present from China!"

Azad felt confused, "When I returned from China, I only told you about how your friend had died."

The parrot replied with a huge smile on his face, "No, this was the advice given by my friends. The advice was how to escape you and the cage in order to be happy. Goodbye, Sir Azad, I bid you farewell!"

**The parrot then took off, soaring high above the treetops.**

Its striking green feathers stood out brightly against the blue sky. The parrot waved back to Azad, then headed off toward China to be reunited with his dear friends. He was excited to continue his life of freedom back in the depths of the jungle and beyond. There were no boundaries for the parrot anymore.

Azad smiled as he watched the bird leave him and his cage behind. He was surprised by himself—he was so pleased that the bird was flying away freely.

*Now the parrot is truly happy*, Azad thought. *I am happy that the parrot is happy—and that is true friendship and true love.*

# The King, the Queen, and the Bee

## A Tale from Ancient Israel
## Retold by Mary Sebag-Montefiore

**This story is a very ancient Jewish folktale about** the wisdom of choosing kindness. It stars King Solomon (the third king of Israel), the Queen of Sheba (ruler of the kingdom of Saba, or Sheba, in southwestern Arabia), and a very tiny bee.

It was a hot summer's day. The sort of day that makes you want to lie down and close your eyes. Wise King Solomon, the wisest king in all the world, sought the shade of his favorite garden, where pomegranates, figs, and flowers grew, and water fell in shining droplets from marble fountains. There he sat on a long chair, yawning, gazing at hummingbirds, butterflies, and bees . . . until the sweet smells and buzzing noises lulled him to sleep. Soon all was quiet in the garden. The great heat had stilled all activity.

Except for one tiny, young bee. She had just newly come out of the hive.

"I'm not very practiced at flying," said the bee. "I must remember what the Queen Bee said: 'Don't go too far. Rotate your wings. Learn the landmarks. Don't collect pollen today, your first flight. You'll be using quite enough energy, and mind you come back, safe and sound.'"

The bee flew steadily for about half a mile from the hive, and then she saw the garden—a paradise of scent and splashing water.

*Oh! Lovely!* thought the bee. *I'll explore all over the garden.*

She began buzzing around the fruit trees, was splashed by fountain water, and, surprised, sank into a lily, which was full of pollen. The little bee found herself covered in pollen, too much for her tiny body, and she lurched giddily from jasmine to iris to lotus.

*I can't rotate my wings,* she thought in panic. *I'll rest in this rose.*

The rose was a pink one, made up of infinite petals. The bee burrowed in among them, petal after petal, pinker and pinker, and very soft. Too soft. Every time she struggled to find a way out, there was another petal.

"AAAHHH" screamed the bee. "I'm in petal prison!"

At last, she emerged, scared and dizzy.

"Oh dear," she blinked. "I think I"m going to

f

a

l

l . . ."

And she did, landing right on King Solomon's nose.

**"OW!"**

King Solomon woke, roaring with pain and fury.

**"Who did that?!" he yelped. "Speak up, whoever you are! You will be SEVERELY punished!"**

*Oh help*, thought the bee. *Now I've done it. I'd better go straight back to the hive.*

Meanwhile, hundreds of doctors raced to the king's side.

"I can't have a blister on my nose," expostulated the king. "Tomorrow I'm going to meet the Queen of Sheba, the Queen of the East. She's powerful, witty, and wonderful. She's heard I'm known for my wisdom. She's going to sail the sea on a golden boat, then cross the desert with a caravan of camels and an entourage of five hundred courtiers. They're all coming to dinner with us. I can't appear with a red, swollen nose."

All the doctors immediately started rubbing the king's nose with ointment, and one had a magnifying glass.

"It's a very tiny sting—must have been from a tiny bee. The wound will be gone in an hour or two, and the Queen of Sheba won't notice."

"I'm seriously displeased," said the king. "How dare it sting me, an important king? I won't look wise with a pink nose. I'll look ridiculous. The Queen of Sheba will laugh at me. Arrest that bee!"

"But I don't know which bee did it!" said the head of the army.

"Then order the Queen Bee here, and tell her to bring the offender with her immediately."

The Queen Bee ordered a meeting of all the bees in her hive.

"I must know who stung King Solomon," she said. "Loyalty and trust—that's what we bees depend on. Which of you did it?"

"Me," whispered the little bee, in anguish. Had she plunged all her hive in danger if King Solomon decided on revenge?

The Queen Bee took the little bee and a group of twelve more female bees, who cleared the way before them until they arrived at the king's court, where they were greeted by people, mammals, birds, and insects. All joined in a loud "Hooray!"

in their various grunts, squeals, songs, and languages as the king sat on his throne, and a very strange cacophony of noise it was too.

**"Be merciful, O King," pleaded the Queen Bee.**

"Here is the bee who stung you. She is very young, and this was the first time she'd flown alone . . ."

"Let the young bee speak for herself," he said. "She should have known I am her Royal master, who ought not to suffer the indignity of a sting on the Royal nose."

The young bee stepped before the king, so tiny that she was hardly visible. As she did so, she suddenly felt her distress disappear, and waves of strength shot through her, making her antennae stand proud and straight, and the yellow stripes of her body gleam like gold.

"It was an accident," she said bravely. "All bees know they must sting when they're in danger, and I thought I was. I fell. I was giddy. And I landed on your nose. Don't punish me. One day I may be able to help you."

The entire court roared with laughter, but the king raised his hand for silence.

"Don't laugh," said the king. "I like her answer. It shows courage, honesty, kindness, and generosity. These are the most important attributes of society, as sweet as the nectar this tiny bee will collect, as precious as the honey she will make. Go, little bee. You are free."

---

**The bee buzzed off as fast as she could.**

---

But she returned to the palace the next day, hanging around the window, curious to see the arrival of the Queen of Sheba.

Amid a fanfare of trumpets, a drum roll, a clash of cymbals, in she came.

The queen seemed to glitter, not only from the brilliance of her smile, the sparkle in her eyes, the splendor of her clothes, her crown, and her jewels, but her entire personality shone. Waves of fun as well as power radiated from her, ready to stir everyone into a state of excitement.

The king greeted her, he and his court at one end of the banqueting hall, she and her entourage at the other.

"All the world knows you are wise," she called to him, flashing a smile. "I'm going to test you."

She produced two bouquets of flowers. Both were glorious, bursting with color, delicacy, beauty . . . Each was made up of crimson roses, white lilies, yellow ylang-ylang with its hanging petals, black irises, and scarlet poppies, and tied with blue ribbons.

"Which flowers are real and which artificial?" she asked. "Don't come any closer. Let's see if you can judge from where you stand."

King Solomon hesitated. They looked exactly alike.

"Can't you tell?" gloated the queen. She loved teasing.

"Give me a minute," said the king, striding to the window, where the little bee was buzzing against the pane. He thrust it open.

The bee flew inside, settling instantly on the bunch on the queen's right side. Here the blossoms and scent were real. The others were cunningly made of perfumed silk.

"There's the answer," said King

Solomon. “Given by the tiniest of my subjects. Well done, little bee, and thank you.”

“Well done, King Solomon,” said the Queen of Sheba. “You are indeed the wisest king in the world.”

“It wasn’t entirely me,” said the king. He knew that he wasn’t completely wise . . . not so wise as the tiniest of his subjects. And to be wise and humble is the greatest wisdom of all.

# The King, the Beetle, and the Silk Thread

## A Tale from India
## Retold by Anita Ganeri

**Long ago, India was ruled by powerful rajas,** or kings. Some ruled wisely, tending to their people's needs. Some cared only for wealth and glory, while others, who started out as cruel and selfish, ended up seeing the errors of their ways . . .

Our story takes place in northern India, in a great city that stood at the meeting point of two sacred rivers—the Ganges and the Yamuna. It had long been a holy place of pilgrimage for Hindus, who believed that bathing in these waters would wash away their sins.

Now, the raja was a mean, short-tempered man. Grandly named Surya Pratap, which means "brave as the Sun," he spent the whole day barking out orders and handing out punishments. He never considered anyone else's point of view, convinced he was always right. There was only person at court whose advice he listened to (though he would never admit it)—his chief minister, Dhairya-Sila.

Dhairya-Sila's name means "patient one," which was just as well. Unfailingly polite and caring, he never lost his temper, no matter how much he was provoked. Plenty of courtiers were jealous of Dhairya-Sila and went around spreading lies about him. The raja took no notice, except to reward his favorite and punish the gossips.

“I am the luckiest man alive,” Dhairya-Sila told his wife, Buddhi-Mata (“Sensible One”). “But how long can my good fortune last?”

Sometime later, the city was gripped by a terrible famine. The raja summoned his trusty minister.

“Dhairya-Sila,” he boomed. “We’re running low on food. Go into the city and seize any grain you can find.”

Dhairya-Sila frowned.

“Your Majesty,” he said. “I will not do that. The people are starving. We cannot take what little they have left.”

“What did you say?” spluttered the raja. “You will do as I tell you!”

“I cannot, Your Majesty,” replied Dhairya-Sila, staring at the floor. “I cannot take the people’s food.”

Raja Surya Pratap flew into a terrible temper. How dare Dhairya-Sila disobey him! He clicked his fingers to summon the guard.

“Take him to the top of the tallest tower and leave him there to die!” he screeched.

It was getting late, and Buddhi-Mati was worried. Her husband had still not come home. Eventually, she couldn’t stand it any longer.

“I’ll go and find him myself,” she decided.

Wrapping her silk scarf around her head and shoulders, she crept out of the house. But where to look? In the street, she overheard people talking about Dhairya-Sila’s fate on top of the tower. There she found

her beloved husband, leaning over the edge.

"Husband!" she called, as loudly as she dared. "You are alive! But how will you escape?"

"My love," replied Dhairya-Sila, "Please do not worry about me. I will think of something, never fear."

So, Buddhi-Mati went home, but came back the next day, and the day after that. Every day, her husband grew weaker, and every day, he told her he'd soon have a plan.

Then, one day, Dhairya-Sila told her to listen carefully. He had figured out a way of escaping, but he needed her help.

"My love," Dhairya-Sila said. "Come back at the same time tomorrow and bring with you: sixty lengths of the finest silk thread, as thin as a spider's web; sixty lengths of the thinnest, strongest cotton thread; sixty yards of the toughest twine; sixty yards of stout rope; and a single drop of the purest honey. Oh, and before I forget, bring a beetle as well."

Head spinning at the strange list of requests, Buddhi-Mata went home. Next morning, bright and early, she went out shopping for cotton, twine and rope, fine silk, and honey. Now all that was left was the beetle. Then she remembered a sweet-smelling magnolia plant in her garden, and found, perched delicately on a leaf, a brilliantly colored beetle.

After nightfall, she wrapped herself in her silk scarf and went back to the tower.

Dhairya-Sila was delighted to see his wife. He quickly told her what to do next.

"First, tie the end of the silk thread around the beetle's body, leaving its legs free," he said. "Dab some honey on its nose, and put it on the wall of the tower, facing toward me. It will smell the honey, but won't guess where it is, and will start crawling up to find it. As it climbs, gradually unwind the silk thread, keeping hold of the end."

Buddhi-Mata followed her husband's instructions, until she reached the end of the silk thread.

"Now, tie the end of the silk to the cotton thread," Dhairya-Sila said. "And let it unwind, as before. Remember, don't let go of the end."

Buddhi-Mata did as her husband said, and the little beetle scurried right to the top of the tower, and into Dhairya-Sila's hands. Gently, he untied the thread around its body, and tucked the beetle into his turban for safety. Then he pulled up the rest of the silk very, very slowly, so it did not break, until he reached the cotton.

"Now, tie the end of the cotton thread to the twine, then the end of the twine to the rope," he told his wife.

And by pulling up first the cotton, then the twine, Dhairya-Sila was finally able to get hold of the rope. Wasting no time, he tied the end of the rope to a stone pillar at the top of the tower, then climbed down it to the bottom of the tower, where his wife was waiting.

"You and this beetle have saved my life," he exclaimed.

"Now, we must put it back where it came from."

Back home, they returned the beetle to its magnolia plant and left it to its old way of life. They spent the rest of the day quietly, taking care that no one saw them.

"No one must ever know how I escaped," Dhairya-Sila told his wife. "Least of all, the raja. He will think I set out deliberately to get the better of him,

and he won't like that a bit."

Meanwhile, at the palace, Raja Surya Pratap was in a foul mood, and was busy making everyone's life miserable. The truth was, he was feeling guilty, though he would never admit it. He missed Dhairya-Sila, his only real friend, and was sorry he'd sent him away. Perhaps he should send the guard to release him? As always, his pride got in the way . . .

Just then, a message arrived for him. To his great surprise, it said that the chief minister was at the palace gates and wanted to see him.

"Bring him to me," barked Surya Pratap.

Dhairya-Sila stood in front of the raja, his hands together and his head bent. Many of the courtiers, jealous of his success, were furious to see him back, but were even more curious to know how he had escaped. The raja, secretly, was delighted, but took care not to reveal how he felt.

"How dare you show your face?" he spluttered. "And how dare you escape!"

"Dear Majesty," replied Dhairya-Sila, smiling. "I beg you to listen to my story. After the guard left me on top of the tower, I thought I was as good as dead. Then, fate intervened. Out of the sky, an enormous eagle swooped down, picked me up in its great talons, and carried me back home."

"A miracle indeed," growled the raja. He wasn't going to let on to his friend, but he didn't believe a word of this tall tale. Desperate to have Dhairya-Sila back by his side, he wanted to pardon him and go back to normal. But how was he going to do this, without having to admit he'd been outwitted, and losing face?

So, Surya Pratap pretended the story was true, and didn't ask any more questions. Dhairya-Sila was restored to his old position at court, where he dedicated his time to solving the problem of the famine. Over time, he grew richer and more powerful than ever before, and more popular. As for the raja, from that moment on, he vowed to rule more wisely. Buddhi-Mata still hoped that one day, her husband would tell the raja the truth. After all, wasn't it far more wonderful for a humble beetle to have helped him escape?

# The Magic Dragon Boat

## A Tale from China

Retold by Shirley Marr

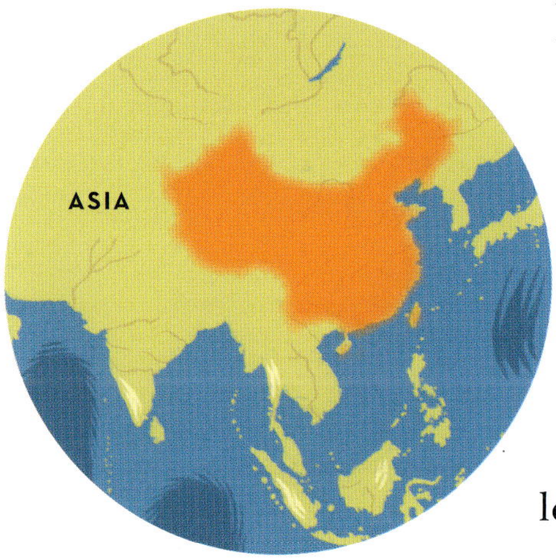


**Steeped in the beliefs of Taoism, Buddhism, and** other folk religions, this ancient Chinese tale forms part of a storytelling tradition that is over three thousand years old. Featuring animals, celestial beings, a boy, and a magical dragon boat, it is a cautionary story that provides lessons in bravery, respect for elders, and kindness.

Once upon a time in China, there lived a poor orphan boy named Chang who had no worldly possessions. He lived in an abandoned shack and worked at a miller's, grinding corn, to earn enough to eat. Yet Chang was rich on the inside, as he had a kind heart. Good deeds brought him enormous pleasure, whether it was leaving what little grain he had for the birds or picking up a drowning insect from a puddle.

In his village lived an old beggar woman whom everyone looked down upon; people would cross the road rather than have to walk past her sad-looking figure—everyone except for Chang. He would always greet her politely each morning on his way to work. The only thing that he detested was that he had nothing to give her. But he could treat her with kindness and dignity.

**"Would you like to be my grandmother?" Chang asked her one day.**

He thought that if he could show everyone that she had a family and was loved, then they would treat her better. Deep on the inside, it was also because loneliness burned within him like an unquenchable fire. For Chang had always longed for a family of his own.

"I would be honored," said the old beggar woman. "In turn, I have a present for you, my grandson."

From her tattered old robes, she drew out a toy; a small wooden dragon boat.

"Now, listen carefully," she said. "The time has almost come to use it. A great flood is approaching. But you must make me one promise: when the waters arrive, rescue as many animals as you can carry, but do not rescue a single human!"

"But grandmother," said Chang. "Won't you come with me?"

The question had only left his mouth when right before his eyes, the old woman rose up from the stone cobbled street and transformed into a dazzling fairy. She leaned over, whispered two phrases in his ear, and then floated up to the heavens.

Chang, startled by what had happened, ran all the way back to the shack. It had already started to rain. The roof was full of holes that he could not afford to fix yet, and water was pouring through. He looked at the dragon boat, which seemed tiny in his hands.

*What good would this boat be, but to ants?* he thought.

He threw it onto the muddy ground. As he did so, Chang remembered the first phrase the disguised fairy had whispered.

**"Grow bigger!" he shouted.**

The tiny boat, half-sunk in the mud, suddenly started to shake. Then it grew.

It grew and grew until it was a full-sized wooden boat. At the front was a massive, ornately carved dragon's head with huge eyes made of pearls, while at the back was a golden canopy. By now, the water on the ground was ankle deep and the boat had begun to float, so Chang quickly jumped on board. He ducked beneath the canopy where, on an elaborate rosewood table, a feast of roasted meats, dumplings, and fresh fruit was waiting for him. Chang's eyes watered in happiness, but not as much as his mouth!

It rained for a hundred days.

At first, the flood was only as high as the top of a person's head.

After a few days, the dragon boat floated past a dog swimming in the water that was so exhausted it was about to give up. Chang remembered the words of the fairy—rescue as many animals as you can. Kind-hearted Chang, who would have done so anyway, took an oar and lifted the dog onto the deck. The dog wagged its tail furiously and rewarded him with licks on the face.

Soon, the flood was as high as the trees. At the top of one of the trees was

a cat arching itself as high as it could to keep out of the water. Once again, Chang reached out his oar, and he hoisted the shivering cat on board. It rewarded him with head rubs on his leg.

---

**In time, the flood covered even the highest clifftop.**

---

In the distance, Chang heard the buzzing of bees that were so tired from flying that their wings were about to drop off. Chang guided the dragon boat underneath the swarm and it settled down under the golden canopy. The bees built a hive and rewarded Chang with sweet, sticky honey. The flood was now as high as the mountains.

That's when Chang saw a man clinging for his life to the last remaining peak.

"Help me!" screamed the man.

Chang immediately thought of the warning from the fairy:

**"Never rescue a single human!"**

But Chang was soft of heart and he felt pity for the man. Putting the warning out of his mind, he offered his oar and allowed the man to board.

The shifty man's eyes surveyed the carved dragon head and saw that the glowing eyes were made of two enormous pearls.

"What a nice boat you have," he said. His eyes moved toward the canopy and saw that it was made of solid gold.

**"I will guard the boat tonight," spoke the man. "This will be your reward for my rescue."**

As Chang and the animals slept that night, the man started to rock the boat from side to side. He rocked it softly at first, so that Chang dreamt he was at home in the shack, swinging in his hammock. Then the man began rocking the boat so violently that it tipped Chang and the dog and cat into the water.

The man laughed. The precious boat was his! He picked up the oar and rowed away, leaving the trio to drown.

What the man didn't count on though were the bees. They stung him repeatedly. He tried to run away, around and around the boat, but the bees kept after him. Soon, his whole face was swollen. The only way he could escape was to jump into the water.

The man might not have drowned, as he could swim. But unfortunately, he had managed to pry off a pearl from the dragon's head. Unwilling to let go of it because of his greed, he sank all the way to the bottom of the water and was never seen again.

Chang and his friends climbed back onto the boat, grateful for their lives. Though there was no land to be seen, and the rain continued to fall, they never went hungry. Whenever one piece of food was taken from the elaborate rosewood table, something else would fill its place—dumplings and sweet peaches for Chang, fish for the cat, meaty bones for the dog, and fresh flowers filled with nectar for the bees.

## After a hundred days, the rain stopped.

The floodwaters began to recede. Soon the land was dry again and the boat came to rest on the ground. Chang headed back to where he lived.

Unfortunately, the shack was in a worse state than he had left it. But Chang swore he would no longer refer to it as a shack. It was now a home. Chang would have a fire going tonight, with the magic food table right beside it. Chang had no use for the remaining dragon pearl or the solid-gold canopy.

There was one last thing to do.

He shouted the second phrase whispered by the fairy:

**"Grow smaller!"**

The boat started to shake. Then it shrank. It shrank and shrank until it was a toy boat again. Chang placed it in his pocket and ran to join his animal friends. Although he never got the grandmother he wanted, loneliness no longer burned inside him like an unquenchable fire.

# Oceania

Oceania is a vast region that stretches right across the Pacific Ocean to the rugged shores of New Zealand and the continent of Australia. Each area has its own special stories, with many showing a deep connection with nature. Get ready to meet Māui, the mischievous demigod of Polynesian mythology, whose daring exploits shape the landscape and culture of the Pacific islands, a bad-tempered giant from Samoa, and a huge rainbow serpent, known to Aboriginal clans throughout Australia, that brings life to the desert lands.

# The Rainbow Serpent

## An Aboriginal Australian Tale
## Retold by Melissa-Jane Fogarty

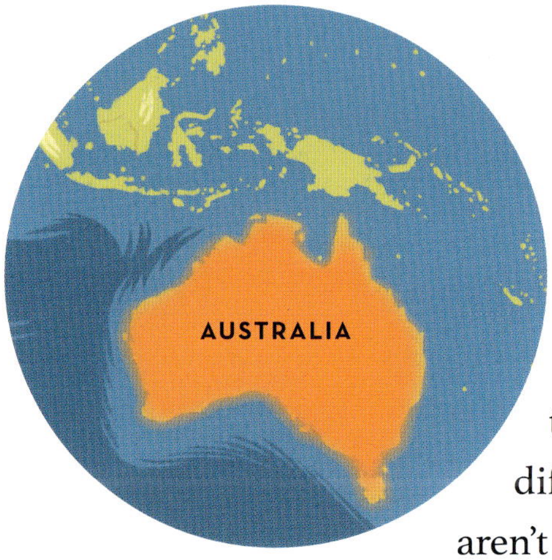


**The Rainbow Serpent is a Creator Spirit or** Ancestral Being known in the Dreaming as a huge powerful creature that created the waterways and brought life to the land. Its stories have been told and shared among many different Aboriginal clans all around Australia. Though the stories aren't always the same, the Rainbow Serpent is often connected with bringing rain, floods, and storms, and also with causing drought and punishing people if they don't follow the laws.

Thousands of years ago, before humans roamed the Earth, there was a huge Rainbow Serpent called Chalahn Dirun (chal-an deer-oon) who slumbered underground. She was so big that if standing up tall, she could reach all the way up to Sky Country.

While she was sleeping in the ground, Chalahn Dirun grew all the animals in her belly. They stretched and swelled and developed as they awaited their birth. Some grew wings and claws, others long tails and rounded ears, while others still grew scales, sleek slithery bodies, and

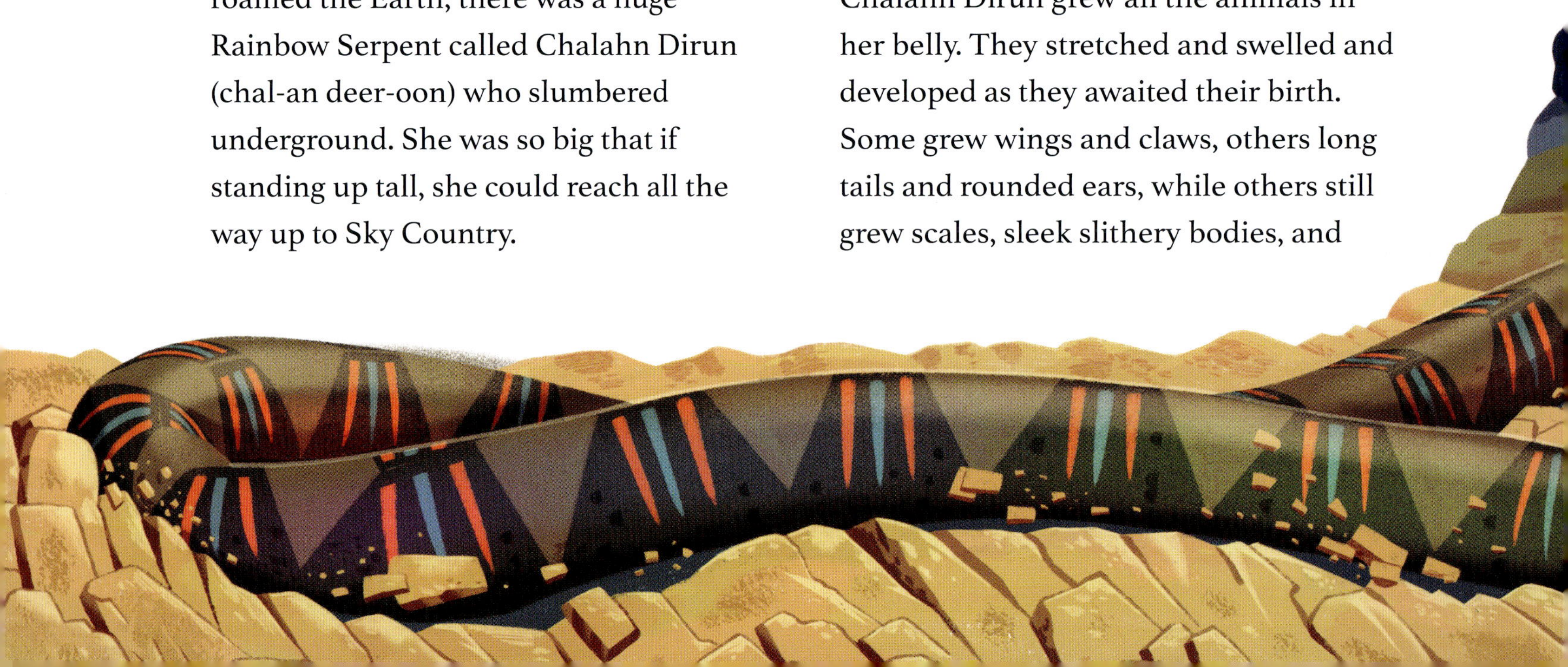

sharp teeth like Chalahn Dirun herself.

When it was nearly time for the animals to be born, Chalahn Dirun emerged from the ground with her big belly bulging. The land aboveground was flat and dry and empty of life.

*This is no place for my animals to live*, thought Chalahn Dirun.

She set out to find a safe place for them to dwell where they would have the food and water they needed, as well as shelter and comfort. As she slithered over the earth, she left deep trenches and steep ridges in her wake.

Chalahn Dirun explored all parts of the continent, from north to south and east to west, until she grew tired and sad. There was no other life to be found—just the dry, barren land now covered with the trenches she'd made on her journey.

She knew she couldn't let the animals out of her belly to live in this barren land because they wouldn't survive. She didn't know what to do. Feeling so lost, she wept and released her sorrow on the land. Chalahn Dirun's sadness and pain exploded out of her in a great, big thunderstorm that lashed the earth until the trenches she'd created filled with the water that rained down.

The storm continued until Chalahn Dirun had nothing more to give, and she lay down on the ground. With the storm cleared, Chalahn Dirun could see the trenches had become rivers, billabongs, swamps, and lakes, and the ridges had become mountains and hills. And with the water came life, as grasses, trees, flowers, and plants began to grow.

Chalahn Dirun cried with relief and on a great big breath she released all the animals from her belly. There were emus, kangaroos, possums, kookaburras, magpies, eagles, dingoes, echidnas, koalas, fish, turtles, snakes, lizards, and more! They all spread out across the land, with some making homes in the trees and plants, others in the water, and some even in the skies.

Chalahn Dirun watched the animals crawling amongst the tall, wavy grasses, climbing the smooth bark of the gum trees, splashing in the rushing rivers, and flying through the blue skies in the glinting sunshine.

**"You have all you need," said Chalahn Dirun with a smile.**

"It's time for me to rest again, but you mustn't enter my resting place in case I mistake you for a meal." And she slithered into the nearest waterhole to sleep and rest after all she'd endured.

For a time, the animals were happy, and they knew to tread carefully and quietly in Chalahn Dirun's waterholes. The animals would see Chalahn Dirun from time to time as she moved from one waterhole to the next with her bright colors streaking across the sky, but mostly she kept to herself.

After many years had passed, the animals forgot about Chalahn Dirun, and she too forgot about them as she slept undisturbed. Until one day, Chalahn Dirun was sleeping soundly in her waterhole when she felt a sharp pain at the end of her tail.

**"OUCH!" Chalahn Dirun cried out.**

She thrashed about in the water but couldn't reach the surface. She'd been pinned down by something sharp and strong. She continued thrashing, swinging her tail back and forth with water splashing in great gushes! Finally, she was released, but a big chunk of her tail was released too. Roaring in pain, Chalahn Dirun turned to see a group of eels and stinging fish fighting over the chunk of flesh they'd torn from her.

Enraged by the pain and by the animals fighting each other, Chalahn Dirun burst up from her waterhole. Her anger and pain reached all the way up to Sky Country where dark gray clouds gathered and burst forth with lightning and thunder and rain lashing the land.

The eels and the stinging fish cowered under the water, but they were not spared as the waterhole swelled and burst its banks. The two groups of animals were thrown into the air where Chalahn Dirun caught them in her gaping jaw and swallowed them all whole.

Chalahn Dirun roared and moved from one waterway to the next at great speed. Her anger only grew as she saw more animals fighting over scraps of food and water.

As her anger abated, Chalahn Dirun could see that the land and the animals were suffering. She'd been asleep so long and the rain asleep along with her that the land had dried out. There were cracks covering the earth, grasses dry and dying, flowers nowhere to be seen, trees fallen and without leaves, plants brown and wilting, and all the animals slow and starving.

Devastated at the suffering of the animals she'd carried in her belly and the land that had once flourished from her powerful rains, Chalahn Dirun vowed never to sleep so long again.

Rain continued to pour down as Chalahn Dirun mourned and wept, until her sorrow filled the waterways once more.

The land started coming back to life after the deluge of rain Chalahn Dirun had brought with her anger and sadness. Leaves were turning green again as trees and plants drank hungrily from the moist earth, the grasses were spreading back over the land, and all the waterways were filling up with rushing rainwater.

*This cannot happen again*, thought Chalahn Dirun as she came up with a plan.

So she made a deal with the animals. A deal that would keep them all safe, ensure the balance of nature and the life cycles and seasons of the Earth.

Those who followed and respected the laws of Country were transformed into humans, and from those humans some were chosen to keep the knowledge of Chalahn Dirun's waterholes and how to find her. Those with the knowledge could approach Chalahn Dirun without harm during her slumber, and when they did, she would bring the rains again or even give some humans their own power to heal others. But the humans also knew that if they didn't follow the laws and look after Country and one another, Chalahn Dirun could stop the rains and dry out the earth, or she could bring on floods and storms and cause widespread devastation across the land.

**Author's note**

The Rainbow Serpent is an Ancestral Being that exists in Australian Aboriginal culture and has done so for many thousands of years. The stories told that feature the Rainbow Serpent vary from Aboriginal Country to Country (there are over 250 First Nations language groups and Countries within what is modern-day Australia) and the descriptions of the Rainbow Serpent vary too, but the creature is almost always associated with water and with giving life, as well as being able to take it away.

The two contemporary versions of a Rainbow Serpent story I relied on while researching are: *Rainbow Serpent* by Dick Roughsey and *Warnayarra the Rainbow Snake* told by the senior boys' class at Lajamanu School (compiled by Pamela Lofts). I also drew on stories I'd heard as a child, as well as scholarly articles from the early 1900s, including these two: "The Rainbow-Serpent Myth of Australia" by A. R. Radcliffe-Brown and "The Rainbow-Serpent Myth in North-West Australia" by A. P. Elkin.

The version in this anthology is not a copy of any other story, but rather my own interpretation from the stories I have heard and researched. The name Chalahn Dirun comes from the Yugambeh language, which was my grandfather's first language, with *chalahn* the word for "rainbow" and *diran* the word for "snake."

# Māui Discovers Fire

## A Māori Tale
Retold by Steph Matuku

**Māui, a demigod with magical powers, was the most** famous of all Māori legendary heroes. He was a prankster, a trickster, brave and cunning, and stories of his adventures are told across Polynesia and the Pacific. His exploits often helped mankind, such as when he pulled up the North Island of Aotearoa from the bottom of the ocean. He also slowed the Sun to stop it from racing across the sky, and as you'll see in this story, discovered the secret of making fire.

Every night, the people in Māui's village put plenty of wood on their cooking fires to last the whole night through. In the morning, they blew on the glowing coals and embers to get the fires blazing hot again.

"What would happen if the fires went out?" Māui asked his mother.

"They don't," his mother replied. "We keep them burning so we can cook our food, keep warm, and see in the darkness."

"Yes, but what if they all went out?"

"Hush, Māui," said his mother, for she was busy as mothers often are, and didn't have time to explain. But Māui couldn't stop thinking about it.

That night, when everyone was asleep, he stole out of his hut and sneaked over to his neighbour's.

Carefully, he poured water on their fire. It went out with a whoosh of steam. Then he went to the next house and doused their fire too.

---

**One by one, the fires went out, leaving the village in darkness.**

---

In the morning, what a to-do! People hurried from one house to another to beg for a glowing ember or hot coal to restart their cooking fires, but there wasn't a spark to be seen.

Māui's mother soon found out what he had done and she was very angry. "You caused this, and now you can fix it. You'll have to go and get some fire from your grandmother, Mahuika."

At the sound of Mahuika's name, the villagers shuddered in fear. Mahuika was a terrifying goddess who lived at the base of a burning mountain. But Māui wasn't afraid. Not only was he curious to see what this Mahuika was all about, he also hoped he would learn the secret of fire.

He took a hollowed-out stone and filled it with pieces of bark to feed a flame for his journey home. Then he traveled through the forest and over the hills to Mahuika's mountain. Red-hot lava spilled over the side, oozing down into the valley below. Old Mahuika sat in the entrance of her fiery cave. Her hair was a mass of white-hot strands, her eyes were like burning coals, and boiling steam rose from her breath.

The air became warmer and warmer as Māui approached her. He couldn't stand too close for fear of melting, so he called out, "Grandmother! It's me, Māui! I've come to ask you for some fire."

Mahuika squinted at her grandson.

"Fire? You want one of my precious children?" she said fiercely.

She rubbed her fingers together, sending sparks into the air. Each fingernail was a blazing flame: Takonui the thumb, Takaroa the forefinger, Māpere the middle finger, Mānawa the ring finger, and Tōiti, the little finger.

"Yes, please," said Māui. "I'll look after it."

"Very well," said Mahuika. "Seeing as it's you."

**She plucked off a fingernail and threw it high into the air.**

Māui caught it in his hollowed-out stone, cried, “Thank you!” and slipped back into the forest.

He looked into the stone. There the flame smoldered, kept alive by the shaved bark. It would last until he got home. But Māui wondered what Mahuika would do if the flame went out. Carefully, he tipped the flame out onto the ground and stamped on it until it died.

Then he went back to Mahuika.

“Grandmother!” he called.

Mahuika glared at him. She liked being alone and didn’t appreciate being interrupted, even by her cheeky grandson.

“What do you want now?” she said disagreeably.

“My fire went out. I need a new one. Please,” he added.

Mahuika grumbled, but she plucked a second burning fingernail and threw it toward Māui. He caught it in his hollowed-out stone and called, “Thank you!” before disappearing into the forest.

Once out of sight, he tipped the flame onto the ground and covered it with earth to smother it. Then he returned to Mahuika’s cave.

“It started raining,” he called to his grandmother. “And the flame went out!”

“Too bad,” said Mahuika. “I’m not giving you any more.”

“But Grandmother!” said Māui. “Without fire, we can’t light our cooking fires! We’ll all starve to death!”

Mahuika grumbled again, but she plucked her third fingernail and threw it toward him.

As before, Māui caught it, hurried into the forest, put the flame out, and then returned.

“Grandmother!” he called. “There was a breeze and it blew the fire out! I’m so sorry. I need another one.”

“This is ridiculous!” stormed Mahuika. “You’ve taken three of my children! Why should I give you any more?”

“Please, grandmother!” begged Māui. “Without fire, we’ll all freeze in our beds!

Our village will perish of the cold!"

"Put some more clothes on, then," snapped Mahuika, for she really was upset. She only had two children left and she wanted to keep them close.

"But Grandmother! Without fire, we won't be able to see in the night! We'll stumble and fall. And in the dark, the ghosts and spirits will come and steal the babies. Please, Grandmother!"

Mahuika tossed the fourth fingernail to Māui and warned, "This is the last one, Māui. Don't you dare come back here again!"

"I won't!" said Māui. But of course, as soon as he was out of sight, he stamped on the fourth fingernail until it was nothing but a black smear across the dirt.

He went back to Mahuika, planning to take the last flame, and then put it out. Then he would finally discover what would happen when there was no fire left in the world.

"Excuse me, Grandmother," he called, but that was as far as he got.

Mahuika leapt to her feet, roaring in rage. The mountain gave a tremendous shudder and red-hot lava spewed from the top like a fountain. She took her last flaming fingernail and threw it at the ground in front of Māui. The fire exploded across the earth and raced toward him, burning up trees and bushes and everything else in its path.

With a shout of fear, Māui took off, but it was impossible to outrun the fire. It blazed from tree to tree, from bush to bush, until Māui was surrounded.

**But Maui was brave; Maui was cunning.**

Calling on his magical powers, he transformed himself into a hawk and sprang into the air. The flames jumped up to catch him, but his powerful wings beat hard, taking him up out of reach. The wind from his wings sent up a shower of sparks, scorching the underside of his feathers red, and he cried out in pain.

Below, the fire roared, leaping into the trees and boiling the streams dry, burning until there was nothing left to burn.

Māui flew home, feeling a little ashamed. What would his mother say?

His mother had already seen the

clouds of smoke on the horizon, and was furious.

"Your poor Grandmother!" she shouted. "And what about us? How are we supposed to light our fires now? We'll freeze *and* starve."

"Don't worry, Mother," Māui said. "The fire went into the trees. Look!"

Then, remembering how Mahuika had rubbed her fingers together to make them blaze, he collected a few dry sticks from the kaikōmako trees and showed his mother how to rub them together, faster and faster, until the sticks smoldered and burst into flame.

**"Now we'll always have fire, whenever we want."**

His mother smiled. "Thank you, Māui."

# Tigilau Versus Seia

## A Tale from Sāmoa
## Retold by David Fa'auliuli Mamea

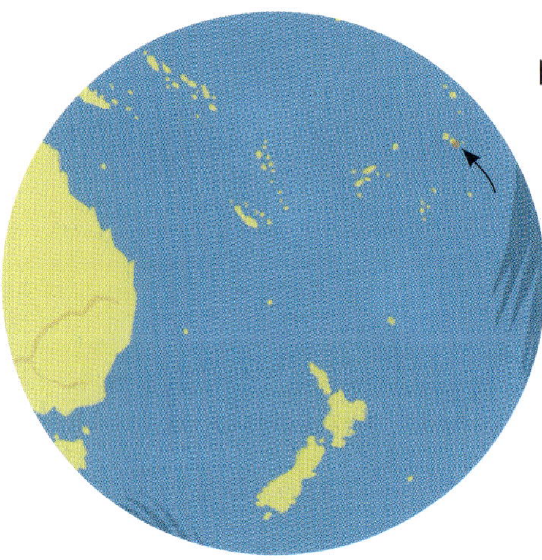

**The high chief of Savavau was a very proud man**—so proud that he decreed that only girls were allowed to be born in his village. His life was pretty good until he heard whispers about a handsome young man who lived at the outer edge of the village. Once he saw Seia's youth and good looks, Tigilau resolved to get rid of the young man—a task that would prove more difficult than he imagined.

Tigilau had achieved many things as high chief of Savavau—the village was prosperous and he had a family with many wives and numerous daughters—but what he was most proud of was his own beauty. No other man in the village was as beautiful as Tigilau, and as the years went by, he made sure it stayed this way by outlawing the birth of baby boys. Families who welcomed the arrival of a male child faced a choice: leave Savavau forever or have their newborn killed.

At the farthest edge of Savavau, on a finger of land poking into the ocean, a young man called Seia lived with his mother and father. He was happy with his life, which he spent fishing and farming and looking after his parents.

One day, a messenger arrived: news of Seia's existence had reached Tigilau and the young man was called on to present himself to the high chief. Seia's parents became afraid. Seia calmed them —he would talk with Tigilau and work something out. The following morning, Seia arrived at the Savavau *malae* (town square), but Tigilau and his family were still asleep.

"Tigilau!" Seia called out. "Tigilau!"

The household awoke to see Seia on their *malae*, his skin glistening in the morning sun, his body adorned by a simple tapa cloth and necklace. Tigilau's daughters were taken with Seia's good looks, their giggles and whispering reaching Tigilau as he roused.

"I have come at your request, sir," the young man said.

His daughters' voices still fresh in his ears, Tigilau saw how handsome his visitor was and knew he had to die. With so many witnesses around, he had to be careful. He welcomed Seia and said, "I am getting old and I need your help. There is a toa tree and its roots are blocking the main road. I want you to remove those roots but leave the tree standing as it has sentimental value to me."

The chief knew that the tree was old and frail—so old and frail that hopefully it would fall on the young man and kill him.

Seia looked at the toa tree and placed a hand on its trunk. Then he set about removing its roots with such speed and strength that he was soon finished.

Tigilau saw the tree still standing, its roots gone and its branches waving in the breeze. Beside the tree was Seia. Thinking quickly, Tigilau said, "You have done such an impressive job , I have another task for you . . ."

"Pardon my interruption, but I must go home to my parents. I shall return tomorrow to see to your other task."

Tigilau knew better than to stop Seia, because love and respect for one's parents is very important in Sāmoan culture. As he watched the young man leave, he swore to himself the next task would be much more dangerous than removing tree roots.

The next day, Seia arrived early and Tigilau said, "I need someone young and limber to collect breadfruit for us. There is a tree just outside the village that is ready to be harvested."

Seia went to the breadfruit tree. It was massive, with long, thick branches heavy with fruit. From up in its highest branches, an *aitu* (spirit or demon) said, "What do you want?"

Seia tried to get a good look at the *aitu*, but the large leaves obscured it and he could only catch a glimpse of unblinking night-black eyes and the Sun reflecting off bone-white teeth.

"I have been sent by Tigilau to collect breadfruit for the village," he said.

"It'll cost you. Since you look as strong and handsome as I've heard, I'll make you a deal. If you can climb up the tree and shake all of the breadfruit off and then be back on the ground before I've picked them all up, we'll go halves."

Seia looked at the tree. He said, "And what if I can't shake off the breadfruit and be back on the ground before you've picked them all up?"

The *aitu* smiled.

"Then I get to kill you and have you for my dinner."

Seia walked up to the tree and touched it. He took a step back . . . and gave the tree a mighty kick! The tree shivered from the bottom of the trunk, where he kicked it, all the way up and out to every branch, shaking the breadfruit loose until the ground was covered with them, and the tree was empty.

"I didn't expect that," the *aitu* said. "But a deal's a deal."

Back at the *malae*, Tigilau looked at the baskets of breadfruit, and at Seia standing beside them. Tigilau's daughters and the unmarried women of the village were becoming quite taken with the young man and his exploits. The high chief would need to take matters into his own hands. He said, "I have one last task for you."

"Forgive me, sir," Seia said, "but I must go home. I shall return tomorrow."

Seia's parents were grateful to see their son come back two days in a row. But when they heard he was needed the next day they cried in fear for their son.

"Your final task," Tigilau said the following morning, is to get some kava plants for our council's next meeting." (In Sāmoan culture, the kava plant is used to make 'ava, a traditional ceremonial drink.)

"You will get it from a man called Uluiva who lives deep in the forest."

He did not tell Seia that Uluiva was a giant who hated being disturbed and had a very short temper. The chief followed Seia into the forest to make sure that, one way or another, the young man would not come back alive.

Seia walked all day in the forest. It was almost dusk when he saw a *fale* (a Samoan house with open sides and a thatched roof) in a small clearing. A young woman came out of the dwelling.

"What are you doing here?" she asked.

But Seia just stared at her. She was the most beautiful woman he had ever seen.

"Can you speak? Can you hear me?" asked the woman.

Finally, Seia said, "What is your name?"

"Oh, you do talk," the woman said. "You should leave here right now because —um . . . "

"What?" said Seia. He turned to find a gigantic man standing behind him.

"What are you doing talking to my wife?" the giant boomed. (The woman mouthed to Seia that she wasn't his wife.)

"Please forgive the late hour, sir," Seia said. "You must be Uluiva. I've been sent to collect 'ava for the high chief of Savavau . . ."

**But before he could continue, Uluiva picked Seia up by his hair.**

"I'm going to kill you, then we'll have you for dinner, and then I'll use your bones to fix my roof."

"Wait," the young woman said. "Did you say you were sent by the high chief of Savavau?" Seia tried to nod but it was

difficult with Uluiva holding him by his hair. "Is the high chief still Tigilau, who outlawed baby boys, and killed those who broke his laws?" she asked.

"The high chief is called Tigilau," Seia said, "but I don't know about the second part of your question."

The young woman turned to Uluiva, "Isn't that the same high chief who killed your parents because they refused to give you up?"

Uluiva brought Seia close to his face. "Did Tigilau send you?" he asked.

"Yes. He has also been following me all day so he can't be too far away."

Tigilau, who had been watching from behind a nearby tree, began to back away when he stepped on a stick, making a loud cracking noise.

The following morning, Seia walked out of the forest with the young woman on his arm. The villagers asked him what happened. Tigilau's daughters and the other women looked Seia's companion up and down.

Seia said, "I met with Uluiva who did not take kindly to my unannounced visit. But we talked a little and then Tigilau joined us and Uluiva told me to escort this young woman out of the forest." (The young woman mouthed to the women that it was a bit more exciting than that.)

The villagers asked who this young woman was on his arm.

"I don't know her name," Seia said, "but I'm going to ask her to marry me."

"My name is Sina." She turned to Seia. "I'd like to meet your parents before any proposals of marriage, thank you."

And with that he took Sina to meet his parents.

# About the authors

DAVID BOWLES is a Mexican American author and translator from South Texas. He has worked on TV and film projects and written more than thirty books, including the award-winning *They Call Me Güero* and *They Call Her Fregona*, as well as a book of Mexican myths, *Feathered Serpent, Dark Heart of Sky*. David presently serves as the president of the Texas Institute of Letters.

FRANCES EVANS grew up in the countryside on the mid-Wales border. Since she was small, this magical landscape and its stories have been a source of inspiration to her. In 2013, she completed a postgraduate degree at Cambridge University, specializing in the literature of the Anglo-Welsh border. When she's not reading books or walking up hills, Frances works as a children's editor and writer in London.

AJ EVERSOLE is an author who writes across all age groups. She grew up in rural Oklahoma and currently lives in Fort Worth, Texas, with her husband and children. As an enrolled citizen of the Cherokee Nation, she is incredibly passionate about supporting Native and Indigenous Voices and works as a Native Voices Reporter at Cynthia Leitich Smith's Cynsations Kidslit News Site.

MELISSA-JANE FOGARTY is a kidlit author/illustrator and freelance editor and writer. She's of Mununjali descent, living on Darkinjung land, NSW, Australia. She has a masters in publishing and is a graduate of the Children's Book Academy and the Australian Writers' Centre. When not sketching, writing, or editing, Melissa is hanging with her husband, two children, and two fur babies, and drinking copious amounts of tea.

ANITA GANERI is an award-winning author of more than a hundred books for children, including the best-selling Horrible Geography series. Anita was born in India but moved to England when she was very young. After university, she spent many years working for publishers both as an editor and a foreign rights manager. Anita now lives in Yorkshire with her husband, children, and rescued greyhounds.

KHAILA GENTLE is a Belizean storyteller who loves to blur the lines between fantasy and reality. By day, she is the editorial director of a Caribbean travel magazine, and by night, she is a fantasy and science fiction writer. What she loves most of all is telling stories of those who, much like herself, never imagined seeing themselves in the pages of a book when they were growing up.

NEEMA GITHERE is a writer and theorist, born in Nairobi, Kenya, whose work explores the cultural identities of people of African descent living in communities around the world. She is a contributing author to several Lonely Planet guidebooks across Africa and a 2023–24 fellow at the Digital Civil Society Lab at Stanford University.

ANIKA HUSSAIN was born and raised in Stockholm, Sweden, but currently lives in Bath, England. She has been surrounded by stories throughout her life and continues to share them whenever she can. She is the author of *Norse Folktales, Myths and Legends* and has also made several TV and radio appearances speaking about inspiring literacy among children from underprivileged areas.

ḴUNG JAADEE is a professional Indigenous storyteller and author of the popular children's book *Raven's Feast*. She has been telling stories for over thirty years and has performed at festivals, schools, and Indigenous celebrations across Canada. She belongs to the Haida, Musqueam, Squamish, Tlingit, and Tsleil-Waututh Nations, and is also part-Hawaiian. She was born and raised on Haida Gwaii and is from the Yaguu'laanaas Raven Clan.

MARIANA LLANOS is a Peruvian-born writer, poet, and translator who resides in Oklahoma. Winner of a 2024 Pura Belpre Honor for her book *Benita and the Night Creatures*, as well as the 2022 Oklahoma Book Award for *Run, Little Chaski!*, she enjoys visiting schools to spread her love for reading.

DAVID FA'AULIULI MAMEA (Safune/Safotu, Sāmoa) writes for theater, film, television, and radio. Born and raised in Te Whanganui-a-Tara Wellington, he now lives in Te Tai Tokerau Northland with his Lovely Wife and their dogs, cat, ponies, chickens, kunekune pigs, and sheep.

SHIRLEY MARR is a first-generation Chinese-Australian author living in sunny Perth and an author of young adult and children's fiction. She describes herself as having a Western mind and an Eastern heart and likes to write in the space in the middle where both collide, basing her stories on her own personal experiences of migration and growing up in Australia, along with the folktales and fairy tales from her mother.

STEPH MATUKU (Ngāti Mutunga, Ngāti Tama, Te Ātiawa) is a writer from Taranaki, New Zealand. She enjoys writing stories for young people and her work has appeared on the page, stage, and screen. Her first two novels were Storylines Notable Books; another was a finalist at the 2019 New Zealand Book Award for Children and Young Adults. In 2021, she was awarded the established Māori writer residency at the Michael King Centre.

BLESSING MUSARIRI thought she might grow up to be a lawyer, but she was born a chatterbox, a voracious reader, and a compulsive keeper of journals. She became a writer. Blessing has published award-winning children's picture books, young adult and adult fiction, and poetry, and has written radio, stage, and screenplays. She believes that children deserve books that are beautiful, honest, and fun and that help us discover ourselves in each other's stories. Blessing lives in Harare, Zimbabwe.

MARISA PASKA is a Brazilian-American travel journalist with a passion for cultural preservation. Her work has appeared in *Lonely Planet*, *The New York Times Magazine*, *World Nomads*, *Canadian Traveller*, and more. When not on the road, she splits her time between Rio de Janeiro and Portugal, mostly surfing, skating, and hanging out on the beach with her son and three dogs.

CLIFFORD SAMUEL is an award-nominated actor and writer of Nigerian heritage with strong Igbo roots. He made his acting debut at the Royal Shakespeare Company and continues to play leading roles in theater and on screen. Clifford is also a playwright and screenwriter, and the author of a series of Nigerian folktales for children.

MARY SEBAG-MONTEFIORE has always adored children's books. She came from a family bursting with books—especially old, old ones from grandparents. She did a degree in children's literature, even more fun than her law degree, and now loves writing for children. She is a best-selling author and has adapted everything from Dickens to *War and Peace*. Her retellings of classics have been published all over the world.

ZARA SEKHAVATI is a half-Iranian award-winning writer. Growing up, she spent her summer vacations in Iran reading Persian folklore tales. She is Lonely Planet's destination editor for the Middle East and Africa, and has written for the *Telegraph*, the *Sunday Times*, *National Geographic Traveler,* and *Wanderlust*. She also writes about Iran to show alternative stories about the country, away from the headlines.

TUUP is an international storyteller, musician, and poet born in West London, of Guyanese parents. He has been retelling traditional stories for more than thirty years and is one of the most inspirational storytellers from the African-Caribbean community. As well as taking part in festivals around the world, TuuP has worked on projects with the British Museum, the Arts Council England, and BBC Radio 4.

## About the illustrator

TEO GEORGIEV is a Bulgarian children's book illustrator, designer, and artist, based in Helsinki, Finland. He loves to draw inspiration from weird nature, rich culture, and little-known tales from history. As an illustrator, he has collaborated with a range of clients, including Penguin Random House, WWF, Habitat for Humanity, and Converse.